BORIS VAKHTIN

The Sheepskin Coat & An Absolutely Happy Village

Translated by
Robert Dessaix & Michael Ulman

Ardis, Ann Arbor

Boris Vakhtin, *The Sheepskin Coat & An Absolutely Happy Village*
Copyright © 1989 by Ardis Publishers
All rights reserved under International and Pan-American Copyright Conventions.
Printed in the United States of America

Ardis Publishers
2901 Heatherway
Ann Arbor, Michigan 48104

Library of Congress Cataloging in Publication Data

Vakhtin, B. B.
[Dublenka. English]
The sheepskin coat; &, An absolutely happy village / Boris
Vakhtin; translated by Robert Dessaix and Michael Ulman.
p. cm.
Translation of: Dublenka and Odna absoliutno schastlivaia derevnia.
ISBN 0-88233-786-6 (alk. paper)
1. Vakhtin, B. B.—Translations, English. I.Vakhtin, B.B.
Odna absoliutno schastlivaia derevnia. English. 1988. II. Title.
III. Title: Sheepskin coat; and, An absolutely happy village.
PG3489.3.A386D813   1988
891.73'44—dc 19   88-14671
CIP

Contents

The Sheepskin Coat

We've all come from Gogol's *Overcoat.*
(An old saying)

1. "How about Going to the Theater with Me?"

It happened a long time ago, about ten years after the first man landed on the moon. Most people have forgotten in exactly what year it happened — there have been a lot of changes since then, although, of course, nothing has really changed, strictly speaking. Nowadays, fortunately, everything's changing without changing, even so, perhaps one or two things might be said to be changing in a certain sense.

For example, if you were now to stand in this city behind the columns of the palace built in the style of Karl Ivanovich Rossi, above which a fresh, red banner victoriously flies, and look closely at the people going into the palace on their way to work, you'd notice that they are dressed in a variety of ways, which is not something you'd have observed at the time of the landing on the moon. Some are wearing locally made overcoats, some imported coats with shoulder-straps, some things made of leather, not from the Civil War years but synthetic. And heads have changed, too: on one you'll see a beret, on another a hat, and even rather pretentious cloth caps on others, while a few — very few indeed, actually — are covered by nothing at all except hair. Change, of course, is staring you in the face, yet there is also no change because now, as before, anyone can see straight away who the more important ones are, and not only among those who get out of a car alone, but also among those who get out of a car with two or three others like themselves, even if not wholly like themselves and even among those who arrive in buses and trolleybuses or alight from a tram around the corner. They have a different gait, they greet each other differently, their heads sit on their shoulders differently. No, it's not a matter of innate variety from natural causes — genetics have nothing to do with it — it's a matter of your appointed position inside the palace. The more important man nods and hurries on purposefully, without haste, while the less important man exchanges lengthy greetings and moves on modestly, not dawdling but not trying to catch up with anyone, either. The more important a man is, the more immobile he is on the inside, and the more confident on the outside, and vice versa.

There had been no change in any of this. Nor could there have been. Nor will there be. Nor will there be!

Now here comes a man in a checked overcoat wearing nothing on his head! Before there were no overcoats like that, or headgear like that, that is to say, none. Now there's a change for you! Although there isn't any change really, it's simply that a man has put on a checked overcoat and put nothing on his head. Where's the change? Now if he were to catch up with that man in the gray hat who just climbed out of that car by himself, and slap him on the shoulder and say "Hi there, Volodya! How did you sleep?" — now that would be a change. But there's been no such change. Nor will there be!

Or take this man coming now — medium height, well past fifty, unremarkable in appearance, but well-preserved, wearing shoes that have just been repaired, and an overcoat just back from the dry-cleaners, not a gray hair on his tem-

ples. Now if this, so to speak, apparently stainless-steel individual were to say to the other, inwardly immobile
individual who passed him and merely nodded in acknowl-
edgment: "Why are your eyes so clouded over at this hour
in the morning? A bit too much to drink yesterday, is that
it? Watch out, my friend, you'll ruin your health — you're
not young any more, you know!" — now that would be a
real change! But it won't occur. And don't expect it!

On this particular morning, naturally, the stainless-steel
man's thoughts couldn't have been further from all this,
and he just went into the palace as always. In the cloakroom
he bumped straight into the new head, the one right at the
top, who for some reason was democratically taking his
coat off in the cloakroom. Probably, thought the stainless-
steel man, because that was the way things were to be done
from now on. He had only just finished thinking all this
when the top man stretched out his hand to him and said
in an expressionless voice: "I hear you're having some
problems at home."

A month before the stainless-steel man's wife had left
him without any explanation — she had just gathered up
her things and left for her home village on the Belaya River.
Her abandoned husband was also from a village but a different village, in Smolensk province. The day before, while
explaining to a young woman poet who had had an
appointment with him why he had such an unusual first
name, he had said for some reason in a state of some agi-
tation: "In the so-called early days, the days of raw enthusi-
asm, my father, who came from a poor family and had
raised his thinking to the level of an educated world-view,
came across the word 'Philharmonia' with a capital P in
something he was reading, and fell in love with this Philharmonia, taking it to be a person and even presuming her
to be the wife of the People's Commissar for Education

since the People's Commissar was so concerned on this Philharmonia's account, and so my father gave me the name I've got."

That had happened in the early days. For one whole day our present political officer's father had kept giving his wife Anna searching looks and then finally asked: "If it's a boy, what will we call him?"

"If it's a daughter we'll call her Anna," answered his wife with some stubbornness, straightening the red scarf on her head.

"No, if it's a boy," said Ivan Onushkin, "we'll call him Philharmon."

And with that he hung a poster on the wall of a photogenic film actress holding a revolver.

"Who's that, Ivan?" asked his wife, who was pregnant with our political officer.

"Philharmonia," said Ivan. "A fearless proletarian, friend of the landless, and wife of the People's Commissar of Literacy; she was assaulted by the White bandits in Zambov."

"Take it away," said his wife. "Otherwise I'll get rid of it."

"You can't do that," said the future political officer's father.

"What do you mean, I can't get rid of what's in my own belly?"

"I was thinking about her," said the political officer's father.

"Think as much as you like, but take her off the wall," said his wife.

After consulting in his thoughts with the People's Commissar, the father folded up the beauty with the revolver and hid her next to his breast. But he named his son in her honor...

"Good heavens, how stupid people were," the poetess Liza had said exuberantly the day before.

Philharmon Ivanovich had frowned. The day before Elizaveta Petrovna had brought him her manuscript of prose poems, which had been rejected by a local periodical; she brought it to him for arbitration. Of course, Philharmon Ivanovich would not have touched a manuscript like that for anything in the world, but he had been given orders by his immediate superior who was hurrying away on leave, and his immediate superior had been persuaded at least to read it and give an opinion by the doctor who was treating a friend of his wife's who was suffering from one of *those* illnesses, at the request of a classmate of his, a chief engineer at a shoe factory — but who had put pressure on the chief engineer was not known for a long time and was not cleared up until much later, during the legal investigations, or more accurately, it was not *who* had put pressure on him that was cleared up but who might have been able to, who knew this ill-starred engineer with whom it all began, that is to say, the changes, although in the final analysis nothing changed at all. Oh yes, that unknown person who knew the engineer...

On the whole, though, strictly speaking, it all began with the manuscript. If there hadn't been a manuscript, Philharmon Ivanovich would not have had to read it and would not have gotten involved in the whole affair... But speaking, even more strictly, it all began with the poetess Liza, who was the author of the manuscript.

Philharmon Ivanovich was not responsible for manuscripts but for theaters and their repertoires. More precisely, it wasn't he who was responsible but his immediate superior; he only helped him to be responsible. But it was always very hard for him even to help, because he was hampered by one innate fault: Philharmon Ivanovich liked all the shows he saw, he always liked them to the point of being struck dumb, of ecstasy bordering on oblivion and complete collapse. He didn't care whether the acting was lively or sluggish, whether the play was clever or stupid, or whether the production was a gifted or untalented one — Philharmon Ivanovich was in self-forgetful raptures over everything, he was prepared to live or die totally with the actors, to feel that he was the Prince of Denmark, a worker in an automobile factory, Anna Karenina, the mayor's daughter in *The Inspector General,* a black freedom fighter, or all three musketeers...

It was difficult, and even painful, for him to conceal how in love he was with each line the actors spoke, each movement they made, and even with the scenery, the music, and the lighting. He would sit in one of the front rows, stiff and motionless; he would go outside at intermission reluctantly, and paid no attention to what was said to him by solicitous directors, *zavlits,** leading actors, box-office personnel, critics or parents of future geniuses. He would walk about the foyer or sit in one or another office with the same immobile face and immobile body as in his seat in the theater, immune to gossip or attempts to influence him, and after the first bell he would go back to his place. After attending several performances he would know the play by heart, mentally prompt the actors, wait with baited breath for words and expressions he knew, and feel real convulsions of happiness whenever the actors improvised and changed the text. His rapture, however, was internal, and not visible.

But he couldn't go the theater too often — people might think that he had been extremely taken with the show, or, what would be worse, that one of the actresses had in a manner of speaking... And he made every attempt not to go backstage either, except when he was accompanying some high-level guest, in strict accordance with protocol. Phil-

---

Zavlit: a theater employee supervising the repertoire.

harmon Ivanovich had never given himself away either by the expression on his face or by the look in his eyes or by any gesture. He would have been glad to sit in on rehearsals and would have been happy to meet the actors, but it wasn't possible... In fact, whenever he was asked after a premiere or a reception of some kind if he had enjoyed the show he would say: "The question's a bit sudden...I have to think about it first, but here you're asking me straight out if I liked it or not..."

And he would give a sudden smile, disturbing his immobility, and then he would become unapproachable again.

If his superior had not seen the show himself, he would report to him: "It's hard to say... It's difficult... I'll have to see, I'll have to think it over..."

Every time this happened his superior would become alarmed and, if he hadn't seen it, would say, "Why beat about the bush? Why do we have to make all the decisions? I'll have to go and have a look myself! Right?"

"Yes, you should take a look yourself," Philharmon Ivanovich would nod. "I wouldn't mind having another look at it and thinking about it again myself, either..."

And his superior always took the bait, always. Philharmon Ivanovich knew that he couldn't resist giving in to a doubt about something and would go to make sure for himself. Philharmon Ivanovich would sit in the theater for a second time and look and enjoy himself to the full, and during the interval he would pay no attention to the worried faces of the director, the manager, or the administrator. After the show his superior would say: "Seemed all right, didn't it?"

"Seemed so," Philharmon Ivanovich would agree.

"Well, it may as well go on. Shall we give it the go ahead?"

"May as well," Philharmon Ivanovich would nod, invisibly exulting. "I'll just have one more look at it, if that's all right with you. You never know..."

"By all means," his superior would say, approvingly.

Then Philharmon Ivanovich would see the show for the third time, confirming his reputation for being hard-working and demanding. In the evening other people went off to their families, to a convivial meal somewhere or to watch television, but he went to the theater. To work. To watch and enjoy himself.

"Well?" his superior would ask.

"It may as well go on," Philharmon Ivanovich would say.

"It's not boring, is it?"

"How could it be boring when it's ideologically correct?" Philharmon Ivanovich would say and give his unexpected smile, and his superior would smile too, realizing that he was joking.

Philharmon Ivanovich's immediate superior changed often — some moved up, some moved to the side, some got out of the game altogether and left the power structure... His previous superior had done something really out of line: he had fallen in love with a large-limbed beauty, a member of a rural delegation from one of the "fraternal" countries. He had married her, handed in his party card when the time came and gone off to this fraternal country where he had settled in a village and started to grow straw-berries, which he was able to do because at that period collectivization still hadn't been introduced there. Some of our tourists once saw Philharmon Ivanovich's former supe-rior in the marketplace there! He was bargaining away in an animated manner in the fraternal language, and showed no interest in his countrymen, didn't offer them any free strawberries, could hardly bring himself to answer their questions, and even refused to have a drink with them. Philharmon Ivanovich could in no way understand what had happened to his former superior, and if he made the enormous effort to understand, his head would start to spin and his heartbeat would grow faint, and so he would quickly stop thinking about his superior, the marketplace and the strawberries and then his heart would once more start beating normally.

On the other hand, the superior-before-last had gone off to the capital to study, and, rumor had it, had done very well. It was said that he had managed to take the fancy of one of the you-know-who.

Because superiors changed often, Philharmon Ivanovich was able to keep watching theatrical performances, with a stony expression on his face that brought to mind a volcano that has never actually erupted, and therefore about which it cannot be definitely decided whether it is a volcano or just a mountain or simply a protuberance on a flat surface.

But this time it wasn't a performance he had to look at, but a manuscript he had to read, and what's more, poems in prose, and what's even more, with the title *Ichthyandros*. Philharmon Ivanovich was not fond of either poems or prose. He had come across the name Ichthyandros in science fiction but couldn't imagine what it was doing in this manuscript, so yesterday he had regarded the author disapprovingly. But she, the author, not content to confuse him with such a title, was also bold enough, entering this light-filled temple, so to speak, to wear a bright green pantsuit, a gold chain belt and a necklace of walnuts. And she also all but called his father and mother stupid to his face, whereas she might have tried to understand their feelings, which were sincere and straightforward. She didn't call them that publicly, it's true, but face-to-face, confidentially; still, she'd done it there, "on the inside," where power is not only exercised, not only exercised continuously from sunrise to sunset and beyond, but where there are no frills, except for the siphens of seltzer they'd put in everywhere not long ago, goodness knows why, all those glass containers encased in metal mesh. There'd been nothing wrong with the old jugs of plain water, without the ostentation and fizz — it was an untimely reform, and in fact, why have reforms at all, they always had been, were and would be untimely. Their head, the one right at the top, had reminded them about this not long before, although they'd been well aware of it themselves for a long time.

"Where can I get something to drink?" asked the poetess Liza.

"Over there," Philharmon Ivanovich said, with a disapproving nod of his head. He signed her pass for her — she wasn't a Party member — stood up and gave her a disapproving look from behind, watching her go to the corner, bend over, press on something, make a loud hissing sound with the siphon and drink, tossing her hair back. And her pantsuit quivered, now touching and giving emphasis, now loose and concealing.

"I'll come again tomorrow," said the poetess Liza, taking her pass.

She knows, thought Philharmon Ivanovich, that my immediate superior told me as he was leaving to settle it in a day and on no account to let it drag on. The previous day he had tried to wriggle out of it and had started saying, as usual: "I'll have to think it over..."

"Think it over," his superior ordered him, hurriedly. "But I want it done by tomorrow."

"And what is your opinion?" Philharmon Ivanovich asked.

"I haven't read it," said his superior. "We'll do whatever you decide. Have you any questions?"

Philharmon Ivanovich did have some questions, but he couldn't put his finger on them.

"What are you standing there for?" his superior asked. "Why beat about the bush? Why do we have to make all the decisions... Go on, get on with it!"

And as he was leaving for his vacation he gave his wife Onushkin's telephone number; his wife called a friend; she called the doctor treating her; he called the chief engineer; he called someone else who remained a shadowy figure; and the poetess Liza called Philharmon Ivanovich. She brought in *Ichthyandros,* and Philharmon Ivanovich spent the whole evening reading it, slept for a while and then spent the whole morning reading it again, although the manuscript consisted of no more than thirty pages but it was like one long brain-teaser.

Philharmon Ivanovich had been thinking about this one long brain-teaser when the top man asked: "I hear you're having some problems at home."

This was a special, unheard-of sign of attention, and Philharmon Ivanovich answered, as was appropriate and as was expected of him, brightly and animatedly:

"We'll overcome them, Sergei Nikodimovich, we'll overcome them!"

He should have stopped at this point but our political officer, having lost some of his self-possession because of *Ichthyandros,* remembered his father and to his own surprise said: "I can't get my father into a hospital..."

His father, now a widower living on a pension, lived on his own, groaning and grunting with his sciatica, and it was getting harder every year to get him into the hospital. This year he had been more or less accepted, but as it turned out there was still no place for him, but his father knew and had grown accustomed to this particular hospital, and felt comfortable there — they relieved your pains there, and your pension kept piling up. And Philharmon Ivanovich thought about this while he was reading the poems in prose, and now standing in the middle of the cloakroom, he blurted out his everyday problems, without going through the proper channels, quite against the regulations. He blurted them out and then fell silent. Hardly had he had time to think what a disastrous mistake he'd made when the top man, who had already switched his sign of democratic attention to someone else, caught what he'd said, nodded again and said: "You must be able to get him in."

This was no longer a sign, this was a directive, and not only for this year but for all future years, so long as the top man was top, even if Philharmon Ivanovich retired on his pension, which was just around the corner anyway, only eighteen months away. Now only a few formalities separated his father from his bed in the hospital, just a few laughable formalities.

Now that's more like it, thought Philharmon Ivanovich, having forgotten even about *Ichthyandros*. This was a change from the previous head who had been unavailable for months at a time, even if you'd had work matters to see him about, not just personal requests, and he hadn't been the only one who couldn't get to see him — even the section heads hadn't been able to. But this new man had decided everything in half a second, just like that.

Attention to the individual is the order of the day now, thought Philharmon Ivanovich, attention to every individual. Here he again recalled Elizaveta Petrovna. He'd made an appointment to see her at ten o'clock, and it was now already two minutes to ten.

The evening before, when he'd read the manuscript for the first time, he'd realized that the local periodical had had good reason to reject it. It was not good at all, he told Sergei Nikodimovich mentally, as he made his way to his own section — it was obscure and ambiguous, incomprehensible from the first word to the last, and the incomprehensible passages obviously had some hidden meaning, although what it was he had no way of determining because the work was incomprehensible as a whole. It seemed to be about a woman who loved someone who lived beyond our world in the depths of some ocean that was a mixture of air and water, someone bearing for the time being the pseudonym of Ichthyandros, although it might not have been about love or about love for someone in particular. Philharmon Ivanovich read the manuscript many times, and eventually managed to pick out one or two passages to comment on specifically in favorable terms. For example, the following: "To head towards you, out of the frothing beer, like a fragment of Selene, and to walk, leaning against you with an amber shoulder, over the cloudy waves, not looking down where those bereft of love dissolve in the dust in doglike satiety..."

It was Philharmon Ivanovich's intention to say something favorable about the Gorky tradition of the stormy petrel in the style, but it was too unclear, individualistic and suggestive.

Or, for example, the following:

"The bus seat had been ripped apart and out of the triangular hole, other people's cares, which had seen stuck inside, came crawling up my back; my back was itching; the conductress caught a boy without a ticket and screamed abuse at him; and you were not beside me, even if just to scratch my back!"

Here Philharmon Ivanovich was prepared to say that the conductress should have been treated differently, that there were so many people still evading their fare, and the losses incurred by the transport system were considerable —people wouldn't pay five kopecks, while in other countries, as a matter of fact, five kopecks wouldn't take you very far at all. Then for some reason he unexpectedly found himself vividly imagining Ichthyandros scratching Liza's back, but this wasn't in the text, and Philharmon Ivanovich noticed that his fingers were trembling, and he shook his head in horror.

Or, for example, the following:

"Ten men went down into the basement where empty bottles and jars were handed in and where there hung a notice in red to the effect that wounded veterans from the Great Patriotic War would be served ahead of others, and they demanded that their bottles be accepted for twelve kopecks a piece, because they were completely empty and they hadn't had a drop of alcohol in them for a long time. They wanted one ruble twenty and insisted they were wine bottles. The black-eyed man serving said how did he know they weren't old milk bottles and he didn't accept milk bottles, and they grew indignant. And my bottles were milk bottles and I asked him what he meant when he said he didn't accept them and he looked at me and said that I was a different matter altogether, and they started shouting that it was unfair, and I said what was a man like him doing in a place like that and he said would I really like to know and would I like to go to another place with him, to the Caucasus Restaurant or the Metropole, for example? And they said, listen, you bastard, if you don't give us twelve kopecks a bottle, we'll burn all the boxes you've piled up to stack all your under-the-counter bottles in tonight, and I said I can't today, I'm sorry," and so on, more of the same sort of nonsense with an unpleasant odor to it. And in reference to it Philharmon Ivanovich intended to repeat what, according to rumor, the top man had recently said, namely that in every district there was a BAM* and in every region there was also a BAM, and that was the road she should take to

---

*BAM: *Baikalo-Amurskaya magistral'* (Baikal-Amur railway), the Soviet Union's most ambitious construction project, in progress now for some decades.

find her heroes of contemporary life — she wouldn't find them by going down into the basements of life.

The two minutes were up and she came into his office.

She was wearing the same suit. But it had become even greener in the past twenty-four hours. Extraordinary how little respect she had! The only difference was that instead of walnuts she wore a shining cross on a shining chain which dangled at her breast, brazenly revealed by the low-cut neckline. Philharmon Ivanovich couldn't believe his eyes; however, he didn't have the courage to look too closely — there was too much breast visible under the cross, she was too white, under the circumstances you just couldn't look too closely.

Frowning, he gave her his opinion, backed up with examples, gave it uncensoriously, and ended up by saying simply: "The answer's no."

Here he fell persuasively silent, lowering his eyes with finality.

Liza the poetess was just starting to note down what he said, which didn't please him, but she stopped almost straight away, leaned her head to one side and began looking at him with her big, gray eyes.

"The answer's no," Philharmon Ivanovich repeated after a pause.

And then, trying to finish with this green parrot who had flown in for an amicable discussion of her poems in prose, which, unfortunately, were not even worthy of existence, he asked her, rewarding her with an unexpected smile: "Are we agreed, then?"

"About what?" asked the poetess Liza. And add in melodious voice: "Philharmon Ivanovich?"

"About the change in your poetic stance and the course you take in your life as a creative writer," Philharmon Ivanovich wanted to reply, but instead he found himself saying something quite different: "About replacing the suit you're wearing in an office such as this, for instance, with the normal clothing of a Soviet citizen!"

"Will we be doing the replacing together or what?" asked the bird. "And what will your instructions be on the subject of underwear, Philharmon Ivanovich?"

The only thing he could do was not hear it; there was nothing else he could do in this situation. Philharmon Ivanovich let his head drop, distressed that this representative of artistic youth would so abuse the advantages of her non-Party status.

They sat for a moment in silence.

"My God," said the poetess Liza.

Then she unexpectedly stretched out her hand across the table and patted him on the head, saying again: "My God..."

And now for the third time this ill-fated morning words came rushing out, against our political officer's will, all by themselves, as if not he but someone else spoke them through his mouth, and moreover in a deep, husky voice, a deep voice he heard as something coming from outside himself: "How about going to the theater with me tonight?"

2. Who's in Charge Here?

That's what he said in broad daylight during working hours, what he said to a visitor who was thirty-five years younger than he, without knowing whether she was married or what her relationship was to his superior, who wasn't applying any pressure but was still making some efforts on her behalf. His head started spinning, his heart stopped beating, the hairs on his head stirred, and then she replied:

"Unfortunately I can't tonight, Philharmon Ivanovich. Call me tomorrow."

And she wrote down her telephone number on a piece of paper.

He could see that her fingers were very fragile.

Later when our political officer was buying his groceries after work, he felt a greenish unpleasantness in the pit of his stomach and, as it hit him, he had no difficulty in identifying as the cause the ideologically lax poetess Liza who had taken his spotless heart and turned it back towards the birthmarks of the past.

"Darling," our political officer heard someone say behind him, but he didn't have the courage to turn around and see who it was and who it had been said to or why.

In the shop they were dropping potatoes of a quality best described as rotten into his string bag and he remembered reading about shortcomings on this front in the newspaper. In this particular shop no change for the better was observable, however. Some directive was needed, but that wasn't his area — it was someone else's, an area in which every year problems arose with harvesting, transporting, storage and the weather. All the same he didn't go to another shop.

On the other hand, the carrots weren't too bad. The meat wasn't too bad, either, so there were good things to think about as he walked along. And in his briefcase there were a few other top-grade groceries he'd bought "inside."*

With a heavy string bag in one hand and his bulging briefcase in the other, Philharmon Ivanovich hurried homewards. The fall was coming to an end, cold and rainy. In fact, it was drizzling lightly now, freshening up his old

---

*In a special store for the privileged.

overcoat and hat. Then he caught sight of something green ahead of him and winced as if from pain. It was real pain he felt in his sunken heart, but not a frightening pain, rather a vague, forgotten one. Next to the green cape, done up under the chin with a gold clasp, loomed a figure in beige with a white collar. Frowning and trying not to slacken his pace or to pay any attention either to her or to his heart, Philharmon Ivanovich kept walking straight ahead, but the patch of green waved its hand in a friendly way at him in the distance, got into a black car with the patch of beige and drove off, turning round to look at him and without any doubt discussing him.

Philharmon Ivanovich had lived the life of a bachelor until the age of forty-eight when he suddenly married a young Bashkirian waitress from a sanatorium where he had found himself spending his holidays. His wife had quickly grown fat and had started to look like a *basmach*,* and being taciturn by nature she had practically ceased talking to him, and it was impossible to say what she was thinking about as she looked at him in her slant-eyed way.

In the evenings she didn't get in his way — this was the time Philharmon Ivanovich liked to make detailed synopses of books on Marxist-Leninist aesthetics, unless there were a performance to go to, and to his joy many such books were published. In thick notebooks with different colored covers (something he insisted on) he would draw margins, number the pages and stick on a square white label with a number, which was the number of the notebook, — and the number had already gone well beyond one hundred. He would write in big, neat letters the name of the book and make a thorough synopsis of it, and at the end of the book he would leave a couple of pages for a list of what he'd made a synopsis of in the notebook. He wrote

*Basmach: a Central Asian anti-Soviet guerrilla in the 1920s.

with pleasure in long sentences, trying to use his own words as little as possible, putting in quotation marks if he hadn't changed anything and noting in brackets the pages of the book he'd copied out the quotations from. He underlined especially important things, for example, things such as: "If there is important things no form without content, neither is there content without form, for formless content ceases to be content. However, form without content may be preserved temporarily, without, strictly speaking, being form, because content always preceeds the origin or development of form." Or the following: "The dialectic of artistic development is such that at different stages in Soviet art moral problems have been posed and expressed from different points of view. However, they have always been indissolubly linked to the ideological purposefulness of Soviet art..." Philharmon Ivanovich used to sit absorbed in this pursuit until late at night, and was not in a hurry to go to bed. He had lost all intimate interest in his wife, making only rare use of her body, and then mostly in the morning, and sensing no response on her part.

They had no children and couldn't have any. Right after registering their marriage, his taciturn wife had suddenly told him her story in bed, with unexpected fervor and in some distress:

"Listen, listen to everything — you're my husband, you have to know. I was only thirteen, in the first months after my periods started. He was a navigator, he used to go up and down the river, and dropped in to our village on leave. Izmail, a Tartar. They all got drunk, he kept giving me more and more to drink, then he stroked my back with his hand. Well, there I was and I fell under his spell, but my mother noticed. She was drunk, too, and she fancied him herself. My father had died. She called me into the barn and beat me and beat me and beat me, and then left me lying there and went off and got really drunk. I just lay there crying and then he came and took pity on me. I didn't understand anything, I was still a little girl, he put me under his spell. Eight months later I had the baby, it was still-born, it was so tiny. Since then I haven't gone with anyone, you must believe me, you must forgive me. I'll be a good wife to you, I'll love you, I wanted to marry an older man. Just forgive me — you won't be sorry..."

Philharmon Ivanovich was so terrified that all his organs grew numb. Everything he'd heard was wrong, crazy — an exception. There, that was the word — an exception, — it wasn't typical, it was out of the ordinary. He himself drank only on rare occasions if at all, when his superiors drank with him and it would have been impertinent not to drink. But when drinking, he'd never stroked anyone's back. He kept his hands to himself and his tongue well inside his mouth. He couldn't even imagine a mother beating her daughter out of jealousy, let alone a drunk seducing a child with the latter's consent. It was this consent which horrified Philharmon Ivanovich more than anything else, — it devastated him totally, although after a long silence he spoke of something else in reply:

"And was Izmail caught and dealt with?"

"He said, 'if there's a child I'll marry you.' He left straight after that, he used to write letters. But what does he matter to us... Forgive me."

"There's no question," said Philharmon Ivanovich, "inasmuch as you were a minor. But what do you mean — he put you under his spell?"

"Forgive me," his wife whispered, and he lay there numb.

According to the doctors she couldn't have any more children.

They lived together for ten years, but had no more conversations like that one. And then suddenly she left him.

After coming home with his string bag and briefcase, the first thing Philharmon Ivanovich did was to feed his cat, who was called Peach, and who had been left behind by his wife. The cat ran to meet him at the door, rubbed up against his legs, quivered its arched tail and waited impatiently for its master to cut up the meat and put it in the saucer. Watching the cat eat, Philharmon Ivanovich for some reason remembered his wife's story, imagined Tartar Izmail's dark hand on her slender Bashkirian back, and an incomprehensible force suddenly tore him away from feeding the cat and sent him rushing to the telephone.

He only became aware of what he was doing when he heard the lazy, melodious "Hello," and he quietly hung up the receiver. Peach, startled, had stopped eating and was watching him. Philharmon Ivanovich noticed that he still hadn't taken off his coat or put on his slippers and that he had made dirty marks on the floor. "Good heavens, what a useless old overcoat I've got," he thought, but his thoughts were interrupted by the telephone ringing.

"Philharmon Ivanovich?" said the voice. "It wasn't you who called me just now, was it? We were cut off."

"I'll call you tomorrow," said Philharmon Ivanovich. "As we agreed."

"At about four," said Liza.

"All right," said Philharmon Ivanovich, hurriedly hanging up, but the telephone then exploded in a burst of rings. "Two-seven-eight nine-zero nine-zero?" asked an abrupt female voice. "A nuisance call was just made from your telephone — a call was made and then the caller hung up. The purpose of the telephone is communication, not hooliganism. In the event of repetition your phone will be disconnected. Is that clear?"

Philharmon Ivanovich was decidedly at a loss to understand how the telephone exchange had managed to expose him so quickly. Forgetting to have his dinner, he started walking about the room, visibly thinking. Now and again he would glance fleetingly at the book, notebook and ball-point pens he had gotten ready, but he didn't sit down to work at his synopses. At about three o'clock in the morning he finally went to bed and fell asleep. Now for the first time in his life he had a completely non-Party dream.

Beyond the village of his forty-year past, on the right bank of the river, there was a forest into which a road ran across a bridge and along an embankment, and in this forest there were many insects, lilies-of-the valley, glades with good grass for grazing cows and even a pond. Philharmon Ivanovich had no presentiment at all that he would dream about this very bridge, this road along the embankment and this forest he knew like the back of his hand, on every branch of which there hovered the ringing of cow-bells, the cries of jays and the scent of lilies-of-the-valley. However, strange as it may be, that's the dream he had, except that in his dream everything looked different and was in a different position: the forest had grown sparse, leaving only small scattered trees, the embankment had widened, spread out like a river of earth down which floated uprooted stumps and piles of branches. There was a smell of diesel fuel, the bridge leaned far to one side, almost touching the water which was shallow underneath it, and the whole earth, the vegetation and the sky had changed so as to become almost unrecognizable. It was an unpleasant sight and Philharmon Ivanovich, screwing up his eyes from the smell of the diesel fuel and the change in the climate, gave, one might say, an order: "Return things to what they were!"

But no one heard him because he was quite alone; only the chirring sounds of a motor saw reached him from the distance. Philharmon Ivanovich walked up to the saw and

asked the man who was grasping the handles furiously like
a coal miner: "Who's in charge here?" The man turned
around without turning off his saw, nodded in one direction and then became absorbed in his sawing again. Philharmon Ivanovich walked off purposefully in the direction
indicated and came to a workmen's barracks on which
hung various posters and faded slogans.

Someone poked his head out of the barracks and then
withdrew inside again, and suddenly the barracks turned
right around and stood with its windowless, doorless back-
side facing Philharmon Ivanovich.

He set off around the barracks but couldn't get across the
piles of wood and heaps of rubbish of some kind. He got
tired, made his way to a spot off to the side of the barracks
and sat down to rest on a log. Then a man in a beige suede
coat with a white collar ran out of the barracks, waved to
him and started hanging out underwear on the line. The
light suddenly dawned on Philharmon Ivanovich — so
that's whose things he was hanging out! His heart started to
pound in anger, and in three decisive steps he reached the
door of the barracks, found himself inside and immediately entirely believed his eyes, as if he'd been expecting
precisely what he saw, a totally natural sight, given the way
in which everything that had happened was connected.

His wife and the poetess Liza, stark naked, sat at a
wooden table, eating potatoes and smiling at each other,
while in the corner by the stove a hunched-up little old
woman puttered in a green pantsuit belted with a gold
chain.

"So," said Philharmon Ivanovich. "That's how it is, is it?"

His wife didn't look at him, but the poetess Liza said in
a soft, conciliatory way:

"Everything flows on, everything changes, Philharmon
Ivanovich."

Her peaceableness suddenly made him feel warm and he calmed down and, looking straight into her gray eyes, he asked:

"We're agreed, then, are we?"

He was no longer inside a barracks and he couldn't make out anything except the poetess Liza's white face and gray, soft eyes, and he slowly woke up, carefully bearing with him as he emerged from his dream all that he had dreamt, everything just as it had been, even the smell of the diesel fuel, but more carefully than anything else he bore with him that white face.

When he awoke he didn't understand where this dream had come from, but the feeling he had was of coming back from an important meeting he had had to prepare some resolution for, and the resolution had been passed without amendment, but he'd put it somewhere and couldn't find it and couldn't remember where he'd put it at all.

"Everything flows on, everything changes," Philharmon Ivanovich repeated to himself in his head, closed his eyes and once more he saw the embankment with the gnarled stumps, the sparse forest and the changed river with the strange bridge, and he realized that everything had changed irrevocably and would not now change back again. No, the wheel of history cannot be turned back on itself, Philharmon Ivanovich thought. There it was — the ever onward moving wheel which not only encompassed the most important matters in enormous numbers, but also rolled on over such trifles as the forest of his childhood and the external appearance of the earth, which had never been repeated and never been restored from the most pre-historic times, from the days of the dinosaurs and primitive communism. He gave a start when he suddenly saw in all its clarity the forest of his childhood alongside primitive communism. At the entrance to a cave sat a primitive woman in an animal skin, hitting one stone against another, while another woman nursed a hairy baby, and in the distance some primitive men were finishing off a ferocious dinosaur in a pit with staves and boulders. Philharmon Ivanovich was lying and dreaming when suddenly someone in the room said in a deep voice:

"A terrible tale without a happy ending!"

He came to and suddenly realized that it was he who had spoken and not just to himself but out loud. He leapt up, ran to the mirror and stared at himself. No, there was no skull looking at him out of the mirror, no werewolf, no vain stranger, but he himself, his accustomed, familiar self. He went back to his bed, sat down on it and mechanically put his hand on Peach, stroked the cat a few times, and then impulsively clasped him to his breast and burst into tears.

3. Don Bizarre Biceps

He sat and wept, and thought that at four o'clock he would call Elizabeth Petrovna and tell her he couldn't go to the theater with her on grounds of ill-health, because now, in the light of the cold, hard day, it was quite obvious that it was impossible for him to go to any theater whatever with her, given his involvement in the ideological supervision of all the city's theaters. Especially when she was so young, and anyway lots of people probably knew her and knew that his wife had left him. There was nothing to do but tell her he couldn't go, but not on grounds of his own ill-health but his father's — he'd say he had to take him to the hospital. Actually, she wouldn't go anywhere with him herself anyway. Or did she perhaps want to exert some influence on him, to get things of hers printed in a periodical through him? What she had to realize was that even if she went to the very top she wouldn't be able to get things like *Ichthyandros* accepted. But if she did go with him, what would she wear? He'd come across women at the theater decked out like, well, virtually like Papuans. She might turn up with a bare back or shoulders and a cross on her almost bare breast. What then?

But the day was advancing, and Philharmon Ivanovich got his father into the hospital, wrote a memo to his superiors about the work being done with young actors and had a bite to eat in the canteen.

And the darker the day became, the more possible a meeting seemed...

The poetess Liza arrived at the theater squeezed into jeans and a sweater that fit like a stocking and wearing, of course, a cross on her breast which leapt out at Philharmon Ivanovich when the person accompanying the poetess Liza took off her coat in the cloakroom — the same man who had been dressed in beige whom Philharmon Ivanovich knew from their meeting in real life and from their meeting in his dream.

The person held out his hand as he met him and introduced himself:

"Ernst Zosimovich Biceps."

Philharmon Ivanovich shook the person's slender hand without saying anything, trying to figure out who he was, but suddenly the artistic director of the theater came bowling headlong into the coatroom, his face a spotlight of charm, and rushed over toward them. Philharmon Ivanovich was on the point of making a movement in his direction when he noticed just in time that the spotlight was aimed not at him but at Liza's escort, a most unprepossessing individual from any point of view.

"Ernst Zosimovich," said the artistic director in an

excited, muted voice, "good evening to you. We've got our top artists in tonight's performance, Ernst Zosimovich."

Biceps gave a faint smile with his thin lips and said nonchalantly and softly so that they would have to listen carefully:

"I've got things to do, my friend, I'll watch it for a while and then go, but I'll be back for the end of the show."

"And do come on to my place, do!" said the artistic director even more excitedly and mutedly. "Hello, Philharmon Ivanovich," he said, finally noticing our political officer and briefly shaking his hand.

Everything, it would have seemed, had turned out superbly — the person wasn't a person at all but a powerful personage, unknown to Philharmon Ivanovich but very well known to many others. People greeted him with respect, making the first move, and he answered pleasantly but avoiding all familiarity. This influential, although to all appearances colorless man, also took Elizaveta Petrovna by the arm, taking upon himself the entire responsibility for the way she was poured into her clothing and for the cross she wore. It was he who sat down next to her in the theater manager's box while our political officer together with the artistic director found a seat behind them in the second row. Everything, it seemed, had worked out well, particularly since comrade Biceps went off with the artistic director almost as soon as the lights went out. But, Philharmon Ivanovich couldn't concentrate on the performance, despite the fact that it had the theater's top artists in it, because he was terribly upset.

He had felt upset from the moment they had met. He realized that his overcoat was quite unacceptable when seen next to what Ernst Zosimovich and Elizaveta Petrovna were wearing. Philharmon Ivanovich's suit was still quite new-looking and smart — his wife for some reason had called it his Sunday best — nothing to be ashamed of at all, just like his smart, well-kept black shoes with their sturdy laces, and just like his shirt and tie. But he only had one overcoat. He'd just got it back from the cleaners, still a lot of life left in it, you would've said, but alas, put beside the beige suede coat of the exalted Biceps and Elizaveta Petrovna's long sheepskin coat with a bright pattern in colored braid sewn onto it from top to bottom, his overcoat was perfectly shameful and beggarly — it fairly shouted to the world that its wearer was poverty-stricken. It was a shabby coat. And he'd imagined that he'd have it turned and cleaned and everything would be all right! No, he couldn't walk down the street beside her in a coat like that — it was unimaginable. Better to go naked, — that wouldn't be so shameful!

"No, better to go naked!" Philharmon Ivanovich said suddenly in a husky, deep voice and then, shaken at having for the first time in his life not sat out a performance in silence, he felt his eyes almost pop out of his head...the poetess Liza thought his outburst was related to what was going on on the stage and laughed.

At that time which, let us repeat, was some ten years after man first set foot on the moon, a firm place in the world of fashion was occupied by an outer garment called variously in Russian *dublyónka, tulúpchik, vývorotka* and *polushúbok.* Just as man in all his variety — and this is something people have to come to believe in very strongly only recently — comes from the monkey, so all these black, brown, chocolate-colored, beige, grey, white artificial leather and real leather coats, genuine fur and fake, with flowery patterns embroidered on them or adorned with picturesque patches, some waisted, some tubular, some short, some ankle-length, some rough, some fine, some with applique — so all these garments which officially were priced comparatively cheaply but sold on the black market for hundreds of rubles, sometimes for a thousand or so and sometimes for fifteen hundred (yes, really, there was a story going round about a woman who paid nineteen hundred rubles for a sheepskin coat, Philharmon Ivanovich had heard it himself in the office workers' canteen) — so, just as the variety in human beings, as many would like to believe, was derived from the monkey, so this many-colored array of garments descended from an ordinary leather jacket, from the age-old sheepskin coat, from primitive clothing, reliable and warm, which any watchman or junior lieutenant had been able to get for himself before. But in the process of evolution and progress the sheepskin coat had reached such heights that Philharmon Ivanovich could not even dream about one. He might have scraped up the money despite the fact that he was helping both his father and the wife who'd run off and left him. He'd have been able to find a hundred and twenty rubles or so, but where could you get the jacket itself? What cashier would take your money in exchange for one? There had been rumors of sorts that people "on the inside" would be supplied but they had not been confirmed.

Philharmon Ivanovich now wanted to own a sheepskin coat so badly that he even caught the disgusting sheepy smell of one in the air, the smell which had nearly bowled him over in the coat room. He sniffed the air; a smell was coming from the poetess Liza's hair in front of him, the smell of a sharp perfume, and Philharmon Ivanovich felt that if he did not right now, this very minute, become the owner of a sheepskin coat he would either die or do something very like it.

The lights came on and the poetess Liza turned her face to him, the very same face he'd seen in his dream, a white face with gray eyes. And Philharmon Ivanovich quietly and with trust said to this soft face with its big eyes:

"I want a sheepskin coat!"

The face looked at him attentively for what must have been at least an eternity and finally the poetess Liza said: "All right."

During the interval she took Philharmon Ivanovich by the arm and spoke to him in an uninterrupted stream:

"I have a friend, an older friend; I've got a lot of friends, actually, almost none of them women, but a lot of men friends; some women friends, of course, but this is my clos- est friend; he virtually doesn't drink, just the odd glass; I don't know what he does for a job, he never speaks about his work, but he knows so much and has read so much and learnt so many languages that it doesn't matter what his job is; he says what he specializes in is understanding. I saw him yesterday; he loves me to come to see him — that's why I couldn't meet you yesterday, he was telling me all about collapsing systems; he was trying to understand why these systems, despite everything and in opposition to all the logic of our conceptions, unfailingly move from an orbit close to death to an orbit less close to it..."

Philharmon Ivanovich was on the point of asking what all this meant, and wanted to say that he didn't understand any of it, that it smacked of something strange and that this was no accident — physics and mathematics and in the case at hand possibly astronomy as well had the right in a theoretical framework to reflect different orbits, if they did so correctly — in a word, he wanted to react promptly, even if there was no point in repeating things to her, but instead of doing that, he unexpectedly announced in a deep voice:

"It's not the orbit that is important but the nucleus."

"Well, he said yesterday," and the poetess Liza looked at Philharmon Ivanovich out of the corner of her eye, "that

collapsing systems have a nucleus of death, which is inside
their orbits, and there is also a nucleus of life which
embraces their orbits. He said there are orbits outside the
nucleus and inside the nucleus and this gives us some
hope. Would you like to meet him?"

"No," said Philharmon Ivanovich decisively.

"A pity, you ought to," said the poetess Liza. "What about
Ernst Zosimovich?"

"What does he do?"

"He's a great lover of the theater," said the poetess Liza.
"It was his dream to become an actor, but he had to go away
somewhere or other, I don't know where. But he's very busy,
he's always being picked up and taken to factories and
meetings and airfields and other places. I've only known
him for a week. It was through him that my verse reached
you. It wasn't convenient for him to call himself so he
arranged it through someone else..."

Perhaps, thought Philharmon Ivanovich, comrade
Biceps is one of those inconspicuous people from higher
up who safeguard our secrecy? Perhaps he's a general? Why
had he never noticed this star among the luminaries and
focal points of power, why had he never noticed the traces
of its gravitational force in the cosmic system of the
regional administration? A bit young for a general... But so
familiar to everyone in the theater — even the usherette
knew him — while he, who had been attached to the theater for purposes of supervision, was totally unacquainted
with him... If he could just make it to retirement...

Suddenly, as he strolled around the foyer with the poetess Liza, Philharmon Ivanovich realized, without a shadow
of a doubt, that he would not make it to retirement, that his
colleagues would not gather for ten minutes to send him
on his way to a well-earned rest, that the most senior of

them would not make the usual short speech, impersonal unless addressed to someone in particular, a speech that in no way sums up your life, but still is awaited excitedly by the departing worker, who seizes on every single word of the summing up, weighs it all, compares it, and wakes up at night later to think in recalling it: "why did he say 'worked hard' instead of 'hard-working' and why did he pause before he said: 'would you mind our turning to you for advice occasionally?' " No, he would not hear a speech like this, he would not be presented with a watch engraved with his name on it, or even a three-volume edition of Cherny- shevsky with an inscription, or even a small bust of the leader, with the immortally wrinkled-up eyes; he would not get greeting cards either for November 7, or May Day or even Victory Day, the most memorable day, quite honestly, for anyone who has fought in the war; and he would be prevented from dying as he ought, while reading his syn- opses in solitude. He would be deprived of his honestly earned lot in life by this chance bird, who for no reason had flown into his dull, well-ordered existence, — but for one or two circumstances they'd never have met at all. There'd been nothing probable about it, nor fortuitous, nor had it been in the order of things, as in that story about a meteorite which smashed through a man's skull and killed him. For no reason at all, directions change — you have to get off a bus in mid-journey and stride out into the unknown where possibly no human foot has ever trodden and there are no collectives to give a send-off upon retire- ment or form a guard of honor at the grave...

While he was grasping all this and thinking, he missed the beginning of the poem the poetess Liza was reading him and caught only the last lines:

The shadows of fear she called thoughts,
After the burial she sighed, held on...
Along a hand which dangled without strength
Like a final burden, ran a single tear...

"Who wrote that?" asked Philharmon Ivanovich.

"I did," answered the poetess Liza. "For a friend on her marriage."

Philharmon Ivanovich felt his head spinning. The foyer they were walking around lost its walls and turned into a marketplace; there was a smell of fish, and he saw himself selling dark blackheads, shiny carp, oysters and enormous crabs. He stopped, convulsively grabbed hold of the poetess Liza's shoulder, and the walls returned to their place. With an apologetic sigh Philharmon Ivanovich said:

"It's stuffy in here."

Towards morning he had a dream.

First of all he smelt fish and then he saw himself and the poetess Liza in a boat, except that it wasn't they who were rowing but a young man in a sheepskin coat, who stood at the back of the boat, guiding it along with an oar. Philharmon Ivanovich at first had the impression they were floating down a river but then, instead of riverbanks, he saw the walls of houses of different colors and heights, with balconies, covered in hopvines and adorned with wild roses; he saw palaces with towers and colonnades of white and pink marble; here and there, covered in the dark green velvet of moss sprinkled with drops of water, flights of steps went down to the water's edge; above the water arched hunchbacked stone bridges and footbridges; and from somewhere came the sound of singing — Philharmon Ivanovich had never before in his life heard either the music or the words, which were in a language unknown to him. Beautiful voices distinctly enunciated each syllable and what they sang was this: "Hostis ut praeceps, tibi domine," and although he didn't know the language, he immediately realized that the words meant: "How beautiful life is, O, my beloved," and Liza too sang: "O caro mio, la bella vita." And this too he understood without hesitation, and realized that they were in Venice, where else could it be, and they were being rowed to the Biennale where he would sell oysters bought for a song from Greek smugglers, while Liza would read poems about collapsing systems.

"Don Bizarre Biceps," he said to the oarsman, "cermente presto."

And he threw him a gold coin. The young man gave him a knowing nod and started vigorously plying his oar. The boat skimmed along a canal above which yellow, blue, green and violet lights burned...

But before this dream he had had a late night. A silent chauffeur had driven the artistic director, the poetess Liza, Philharmon Ivanovich and comrade Biceps in a black car... Ernst Zosimovich himself had invited Philharmon Ivanovich to join them in the car, and the director had said he was very pleased he could come, unless, of course, it was too late for comrade Onushkin, but if not then he'd of course be delighted to have an unexpected guest join them. And so they arrived and went up to the director's apartment where there were already masses of people and where Philharmon Ivanovich was greeted by the astonished manager of the city's largest secret enterprise, a man he already knew, and other faces he knew or half knew kept popping up around him. From the wall a carving of the god Sabaoth glared down at them, and from the ceiling hung bells and chimes, tinkling at different pitches whenever anyone's head hit them. Above the kitchen window hung a real ship's wheel with a shiny, highly polished bronze finish. Philharmon Ivanovich found himself at an enormously long oval table beside an old actress he knew well, although she didn't know him at all, and he succeeded in drinking almost nothing and in saying nothing at all, and no one asked him to. The place was full of people wanting to drink and propose toasts. The director had become preoccupied and kept going out to get bottles from somewhere, but they were emptied instantly and he didn't even have time to sit down. Then comrade Biceps came up to him, asked him something and made his way to the telephone which was right behind Philharmon Ivanovich, so that the latter couldn't help hearing what this puny yet powerful man was saying.

"This is Biceps speaking. Bi·ceps. Who's on duty there today? Put him on, would you. Anatoly, I want you to go to Yelena Ivanovna's and get a case of the Armenian cognac and some lemons. I particularly want some lemons and the rest you can work out yourself. Have it put down to me... Then get over here. Yes, I'm with the actors. I'll give you twenty minutes and not a second more."

Philharmon Ivanovich was, of course, aware that in the interests of building communism in general it was some-times justifiably necessary to violate the moral code of indi-vidual builders. But for someone to order food and drink like this in the middle of the night — through Yelena Ivanovna who was in charge of the residence for special guests, both local and foreign — and in front of everyone, party members and outsiders, when there could be no thought of there being any pardonable reason or even any grounds whatsoever — people were just relaxing in a pri-vate manner, the way people relaxed every night — for it to be done just like that, as simply as spitting — Philharmon Ivanovich couldn't even have imagined before this that anyone had such power. And when exactly twenty minutes later the director started dealing bottles of cognac onto the table like cards, calling them "fixes," Philharmon Ivanovich started drinking glass after glass, feeling with some enjoy- ment that in doing so he was in some measure rescuing what belonged to the people from senseless plundering.

The gray-haired actress, laughing like a child, was telling him that comrade Biceps whose profession, speaking bluntly, was rather unclear, was nonetheless a sensitive, kindly man who had nothing to do with, you know, tele- phone tapping or anything like that — that wasn't the sort of thing he was involved in. He liked telling jokes and the things he came out with sometimes! I asked him, said the gray-haired actress, laughing, come on, tell me, what *do* you really do, come on, how do you come to have all those connections and opportunities, and he told me in great secret that someone had to protect something or other from something that could possibly occur somewhere or other, do you understand? So that's who he is, and some- times he's not averse, himself, to saying things he shouldn't — only he doesn't like drinking much, just a little, you know, purely symbolically. Yet he can drink as much as you like and you'd never notice a thing, don't worry about how thin he is, I don't know how he keeps going. They probably teach them specially how to do it, what do you think? Did they teach you how to, for example, or are you self-taught? And he's so thoughtful, he's gotten apartments for so many actors, and he even — said the actress, in tears — got my son out of military service. There was no one who could help, but he went to see someone and my son stayed at home. I just don't know how to repay him, I can't think of anything — what would you advise, how do people thank people like him?

Then the poetess Liza came up to Philharmon Ivanovich

and took him by the arm and led him over to comrade Biceps, who was wearily noting something down in a little gold-rimmed black book while the manager of the secret enterprise stood over him and said insistently:

"Ernie, I need this type of steel desperately, I just have to have it. Our quotas are exhausted and there are still two months to the end of the year. I want you to understand, Ernie..."

"I've written it down," said Biceps. "Anything else?"

"They won't let me have Nyangizayev..."

"That's a different republic, a different Council of Ministers," said Biceps, thinking. "Alright, I'll go out and take a little walk tomorrow at twelve. Have a car wait for me by the monument... At precisely twelve o'clock!"

"I'll pop over there myself!" said the manager joyfully.

"Is that all for you, Rem?"

"We'll have a talk tomorrow, there are just one or two other things, nothing important."

"Well, enjoy yourself, Rem, have a dance, you're putting on a bit of weight...!"

Philharmon Ivanovich had heard about Nyangizayev. Someone very high up had been agitating to get him for a long time but they wouldn't agree to it at the top. Yet here was comrade Biceps...

"And what can I do for you, Elizaveta Petrovna?" asked comrade Biceps.

"We need a sheepskin coat," said the poetess Liza, sitting down on the arm of his chair and nodding at Philharmon Ivanovich.

"What do you need it for?" Biceps asked him gently.

"Is it really true that they taught you to drink without getting drunk?" Philharmon Ivanovich blurted out in a deep voice.

"Fairy stories, my dear Philharmon Ivanovich," Biceps

replied. "Terrifying fairy stories without a happy ending. Please sit down, here's a chair."

The poetess delicately moved away.

"I don't want to," said Philharmon Ivanovich.

"A sheepskin coat is not a problem," said Biceps. "Half the theater wears sheepskin coats I got for them. The director already has three of them. But it's of no help to him, Philharmon Ivanovich, either as an artist or as a man. Of no help... But do sit down."

"I don't want to," said Philharmon Ivanovich and sat down.

"I love the theater more than anything in the world," said Biceps with a touch of melancholy. "And all of us are players in it... And you?"

"Yes," said Philharmon Ivanovich and burst into hearty laughter, throwing back his head. Biceps looked at him, gave a thin-lipped smile, shook his head with a mixture of reproach and satisfaction and said in a colorless voice:

"For instance, he's going to put on Gogol. But you ask him what his idea of Gogol is. Have you asked?"

"No."

"Do you want me to?"

And Biceps did ask him and the director answered at some length but what exactly he said Philharmon Ivanovich could not understand at the time or remember afterwards.

"See?" Biceps asked rhetorically when the director had moved away. The poetess Liza rolled up a little table on wheels with cognac and lemons on it and disappeared with a wave of her hand.

"He thinks he's going to put on *The Inspector General*... Three sheepskin jackets. All of them through me... Yet he doesn't have any idea of what real power is, sacred or profane... In Gogol's plays not a single gun goes off, not ever!

But it's not just a matter of guns. Would you like me to get you a gun? With your name engraved on it? A lot of people want me to... Let's drink, Philharmon Ivanovich, to Gogol. He was the cleverest man in Russia. He ran away to Italy, they say, to get away from his fellow countrymen... The trouble was you couldn't have an Inspector General in Italy. There, my dear Philharmon Ivanovich, you had the Venetian Moor, Goldoni and the Duke knows who else.. Let's have a drink, my friend, for we're no less great artists than they. Excuse me, they're sidling up to me again. Duke forgive them... No, no, don't get up, please!"

This time Biceps was asked for a garage and a place to put it and he wrote a note to someone or other. Then he and Philharmon Ivanovich drank to the theater. Philharmon Ivanovich's authority was growing by the minute from his proximity to such a man. Biceps wrote down a request to get someone a car, a Zhiguli which could only be dark coffee-colored with a nacreous finish. He drank to the theater again, guaranteed someone's wife a place in a sanitorium for the elite near Sochi, drank to the theater again, wrote down the measurements of some foreign eye-glass frames for someone, had another drink, guaranteed someone else a supply of galvanized iron and a boiler for their dacha, and drank to the theater again — each time clinking glasses with Philharmon Ivanovich. Then Philharmon Ivanovich heard everyone shouting "hurrah" in Biceps' honor and singing him a gypsy song of welcome, and then he found himself being handed over to the silent chauffeur and told by way of farewell to bring seventy-three rubles to the monument at five minutes to twelve with a note giving his size and height, and also his address, and to be home the next night after seven o'clock for the delivery. At home Philharmon Ivanovich went to sleep and dreamt, naturally, of Venice.

Philharmon Ivanovich stroked Peach. The cat smelled of a sharp perfume, and Philharmon Ivanovich's heart stopped in fright until he realized that this was the hand by which the poetess Liza had led him to Biceps. He dialed her number, but no one answered although he let it ring for about ten minutes. Then he took the money, put it in an envelope, wrote down his size, height and address and hurried out. It was half raining and half snowing, which made him feel a rush of violent joy. He went to a phone and called the secretary of his section and told her in a deep voice that he'd caught a cold and would go straight to the House of Culture and would be in after twelve. However, he didn't go to the House of Culture but to an apartment block.

He didn't use the lift — it might have broken down all of a sudden — but walked up to the tenth floor and rang the musical door-chimes. He rang for a long time and insistently. Eventually he heard footsteps on the other side of the door.

"Who is it?" asked the voice of the poetess Liza.

"Please let me in," said Philharmon Ivanovich.

Once inside the entrance hall of her apartment he looked first at her, encased in her jeans and sweater like a stocking, and then at the beige suede coat with the white collar, hanging on a coat-hanger, and then he looked round at his own, Philharmon Ivanovich's, dirty footprints in the doorway and said with trembling lips:

"Can I have something to write with, please, Elizaveta Petrovna?"

When he had the pencil, he took out the crumpled envelope and added four words underneath the address: "black, at least dark-colored" and held out the envelope to the poetess Liza who all this time had not said a word.

"You ask him, Elizaveta Petrovna, so I don't have to go at

five to twelve, I really can't today, Elizaveta Petrovna..."

At work he wandered around looking into various offices and he even went downstairs about ten times to the vestibule where the militiaman was standing checking people in and out, and at five to twelve he stood at his window from which he had a good view of the monument. The black car was already standing beside the monument and near it the manager of the secret enterprise was pacing up and down. At precisely twelve o'clock Biceps appeared, he and the manager embraced, got into the car and drove off.

Philharmon Ivanovich stood at the window for a long time, evidently lost in thought.

"But he doesn't cause anyone any harm!" Philharmon Ivanovich suddenly said in a deep voice and burst into deafening loud laughter, but straight away fell silent and looked around, opening his eyes widely.

Just then the section secretary looked in, wearing a "fancy loaf" hairdo on a head almost ready for retirement. She guarded both personal and social secrets behind the impassivity of her face. She stared at the startled Philharmon Ivanovich and asked:

"Are you alone?"

"I've got a cough," said our party official, shattered.

"There have been no calls for you," — and the secretary slammed the door.

But immediately there was a ring.

"Please call by for me this evening," said the poetess Liza, "we'll go to a party, please do come..."

"After seven..." he started to say.

"It doesn't matter if it's at one in the morning! Please do come, though, I really want you to, I'm going to read some of my poems."

"I'll try," he said.

"You'll come, then?"

"Uh-huh," he agreed and, still not hanging up, he again for some reason burst into laughter, quickly fell silent and started listening, but the secretary kept on typing and didn't come into his office again. Our political officer felt, of course, that something was wrong with him, but he didn't dwell on it.

By evening it had become quite cold and it was snowing properly. Philharmon Ivanovich, who during the day had had fantasies of warm weather, a bright sun, a clear sky and other things rarely encountered in the city, became excited. Violent joy seized him again, making it intolerable to wait, and by twenty to seven he was simply walking up and down the corridor of his apartment near the door — up to it and away from it, up to it and away from it. At precisely seven o'clock there was a ring. At that moment Philharmon Ivanovich was by the door and opened it as the ring was still sounding...

"Comrade Onushkin?" asked the young, taciturn man. "This is for you." And he handed him a large parcel bound with ordinary string.

"Do I sign for it? How much do I owe you for the delivery?" Philharmon Ivanovich mumbled, taking the parcel.

4. "Full name?"

But the young man was already hurrying away without uttering even a syllable in reply.

"Thank you," said Philharmon Ivanovich softly, listening carefully. The main door banged and then there was the roar of a powerful motor. Philharmon Ivanovich went back into his apartment without drawing the bolt, put the parcel on the table and cut the string.

On the table, its sleeves thrown back as if it were about to embrace him, sprawled the new sheepskin coat, a dark chocolate color with light-colored fur and round, black buttons. Philharmon Ivanovich put it on. It didn't pinch anywhere. He looked in the mirror, straightening his shoulders and holding his head up high. He naturally didn't hear the front door open and close or someone come into the room behind him. It was only when he glimpsed a movement in the mirror that he turned completely around like the hero in a cowboy film. Before him stood not a thief, not a robber, not an enemy, but the poetess Liza in a short gray fur coat of extraordinary charm, a squirrel-fur hat and high boots.

"I took a cab," she said.

"I'm ready," he said.

The only doubts he had concerned his hat, a fairly old one, worn down to the leather at the back, although no one would ever notice it, but the top was all right, it was brown, and, anyway, once in the taxi he could hold his hat in his hand.

There were few sheepskin coats to be seen on the street. There were far more overcoats like his old one which had now totally outlived its usefulness and should be thrown out. His attention was leaping from one thing to another and was least of all attracted by the poetess Liza's beauty. At one and the same time he was observing how people were dressed and thinking about what awaited him. The usual thought passed through his mind that people were dressed much better than just after the war or ten years ago, but before this thought could take firm shape in words or figures, it somehow gave a sort of guilty laugh and disappeared. All he could do was blink in a vexed fashion as he watched it go. He also thought with alarm about what she was wearing under her coat and what everyone else would be wearing under their coats and, above all, how they would behave. He'd heard rumors about modern-day youth, how they sometimes watched underground pornographic films and how striptease shows sometimes took place. His colleagues with some knowledge of what was going on attacked such films and striptease shows in the appropriate circumstances, but as they did so sometimes allowed themselves to wink at it. And now various pictures began to pass before Philharmon Ivanovich, each one more interesting than the other. He saw, for instance, something which was not exactly tobacco smoke and not exactly steam either, and then modern-day youth, all of whom were very scantily dressed. A monkey-like young man wearing red swimming-trunks pushed a full-breasted girl with closed eyes higher and higher on a swing. From one corner blared revolting, wordless music, and from the other corners hostile voices resounded. A fat girl in glasses crawled out of one of the next rooms, carrying an unbelievably thin girl on top of her who was smacking her across the bottom with a theater program and shouting that no country could bring happiness to mankind if there were shortages of everything, even toilet paper. Philharmon Ivanovich screwed up his eyes, shook his head and said to the poetess Liza:

"Don't use my name when you're talking to me tonight."

"A person's name is inseparable from the person," the poetess Liza objected.

"Just for tonight," he said, opening his eyes.

A taxi stopped at some traffic lights and Philharmon Ivanovich started back; he found himself staring almost straight into the face of one of the top men in his department, not the very top man but still someone very high up who, having noticed the beauty of the poetess Liza, had stopped slumping in his seat and looked out of the window of his car at her and even opened it a little, despite the cold. Then he transferred his gaze to Philharmon Ivano-vich's coat, trying himself out in his position beside such beauty, suddenly realizing who it was wearing the coat. The highly placed personage was not able to disguise his amaze-ment, although someone of the rank he had attained ought not properly to have given open expression to such feel-ings. Philharmon Ivanovich did not have time to greet him respectfully, as was proper for someone of his rank, even if it was after he had been recognized instead of straight away, which was the only correct thing to do, but he did not have time because the lights turned green and the highly placed personage was borne away with his neck twisted round and a look of amazement on his face.

"Actually, I think he was just wearing an overcoat," was all Philharmon Ivanovich could come out with and the poet-ess Liza summed everything up out of the corner of her eye.

Under her fur coat the poetess Liza turned out to be wearing a long and totally severe dress with flowers on it, although on the right hand side there was a slit from the floor to her waist. But the slit didn't reveal everything and then not all the time. There were no naked people there, in fact, the only people there were the host and his wife, a very young couple, and there wasn't even any vodka, just dry white wine.

The poetess Liza read her poem in the same voice she spoke in — melodious with a note of husky indolence.

> In people's games there's a limit —
> Here the game dies.
> It grows quiet.
> Like a shooting-gallery

When they change the targets,
Like the world
When a decision is taken.
Like the sea
When, fallen overboard, you watch the ship sail on
And know you'll call in vain.
Like a morgue
Where you fail to find your loved one,
Like the stupor
Of drunken dreams you lose your thoughts in.
In people's games there's a limit —
Here the game dies.

"Who's that about?" thought Philharmon Ivanovich. She also read this one:

A line in a letter, a handful of words —
It's simpler than simple to scribble that.
A door. And every ring at it
Is like an executioner's gun misfiring.
Another wait. Fragile fingers.
For a line in a letter, a handful of words.

No doubt about it, she has fragile fingers, thought Philharmon Ivanovich, and he began to quiver slightly as people do from severe cold or drinking too much.

Then they talked and Philharmon Ivanovich had a feeling of confidence because he kept remembering all the time about his sheepskin coat hanging in the entrance hall and for this reason he confidently expressed his point of view on the poems:

"For many people their fate and their poetry are separate things, despite their talent. That's your case too. It's immaturity."

The poetess Liza's eyes narrowed and she said, "Wasn't it you who returned *Ichthyandros* to me?"

"It was," said Philharmon Ivanovich. "That's what it's like for you, Elizaveta Petrovna, your fate is separate..."

"Separate from what?"

"From everything, Elizaveta Petrovna, from you yourself, for example..."

"And what about Ernst Zosimovich?" asked the poetess Liza.

"Let's not discuss comrade Biceps, Elizaveta Petrovna," said Philharmon Ivanovich, seeing the light with unexpected finality. "Not now..."

He could feel his heartbeat in his temples and a warmth in his cheeks from inside and he spoke quickly and eagerly. For example, his hostess said of some people he didn't know:

"He can't live with her and she can't live with him, yet for some reason they go on living together..."

And he explained:

"The reason no outsider can sort out another couple's situation is not that the details of the husband's and wife's relations are insufficiently well known but that the husband and wife themselves don't fully understand their relations to each other, and if they can't untangle it all, how on earth can an outsider?"

"But what if they're not yet husband and wife?" asked the host.

"How can you untangle it all?" asked the poetess Liza.

"Here you are still young, yet you don't know," said Philharmon Ivanovich, remembering his sheepskin coat, "that the only thing that can untangle anything is love."

"Were you christened?" asked the poetess Liza.

"My father stood guard over my cradle with a rifle in his hands," he answered, "so as to prevent the enactment of that vile ritual. But his vigilance slipped, his mother-in-law got him drunk, kidnapped me and defiled me, as he explained it. What they named me I don't know..."

"My God," said the poetess Liza. "How ridiculous people were."

And Philharmon Ivanovich did not take offense but smiled to himself with his disarming smile because he remembered how his father always used to say:

"I never let go of my unbending optimism, even when the barrel of a gun was pointing at me as I stood before the firing-squad, and I often stood before the firing-squad."

"Why do you sometimes talk in a deep voice?" asked the poetess Liza.

"There's something the matter with my throat," answered Philharmon Ivanovich, remembering his sheepskin coat.

"Give me a call," said the poetess Liza as they said good-bye.

He stood in the doorway with his hat in his hand, straightening his shoulders beneath his sheepskin coat and again could see nothing but the poetess Liza's wide-open face. Then his face hurried to her face, his eyes closing. He pressed up against it and for one second felt her eyebrow, cheekbone, nose, the corner of her lips — her eyebrow with his eyebrow, her cheekbone with his nose, the corner of her lips with the corner of his lips — and then he turned away and left.

"I felt such joy with you tonight," he said once in the street as he put his hat on with both hands.

Towards morning he had a dream:

Across the river in his forty-year-old past, near the forest, there was a pond and there he was, standing after sunset on the bank of the pond looking at its dark surface, across which were floating white lilies, the very same ones, as he had recently learnt from the press, that had been entered into the Red Book of the world's endangered plants and animals. He looked at them and thought how sad it was that they were dying out, and how it was actually high time some decision were taken concerning changes to be made. And the lilies were growing whiter, and the water beneath them was shining bright and becoming more transparent, and now the whole pond had become transparent, and then he perceived that the lilies weren't lilies at all and that they weren't floating on the water but were sitting on the bank and had light-colored heads and hands, and that they were children, and as a matter of fact he seemed to know some of them. They weren't wearing pioneer scarves, there was no sign of any leader or teacher or indeed of any grown-ups at all, and how these children in white shirts had gotten here he had absolutely no idea.

Then his wife came out of the pond and spoke to him through tears as she walked past him towards the forest:

"You've forgotten everything, these are children who didn't have time to be christened. You'll never be forgiven that sin, and my child isn't even here."

When she got to the edge of the forest she got into a black car with Biceps who said to her:

"I thought you were never coming, Duke forgive you."

And they drove away, and then one of the boys came up to Philharmon Ivanovich and said:

"Take me home with you, please take me home. I want to live with you."

"What about the others?" Philharmon Ivanovich asked.

"They don't want to," said the boy.

Philharmon Ivanovich carried him, warming him against his chest under the edges of his jacket and the boy said:

"Bring me back here in a year and we'll say good-bye to each other. I'll live with you, but take care no one sees me. No one must see me, think of somewhere to put me."

Philharmon Ivanovich's house turned out to be very suitable in this regard. It had a large Russian stove with little windows in it — he'd lived in one just like it when he'd been a child, but in his dream he lived in it all alone. He put the boy on top of the stove, drew the curtain, let him out for a walk at night, fed him, read him books, and told him stories.

Everything would've been fine if Peach hadn't shied away from the boy, and almost run away altogether. He would come home only now and then, looking skinny, and eat voraciously; he would hiss at the stove, arching his back, his fur standing on end. The boy would peep out and call to him to come and play, but Peach would back towards the door and make off.

Once there was a gathering at Philharmon Ivanovich's of all his relatives, among whom was Liza, to celebrate some public holiday or other — it might have been New Year's or Christmas or Easter, it wasn't clear to him in his dream. They were all sitting at one table, eating and drinking and talking a lot. His wife and Liza gave a very beautiful rendition in two voices of this song:

> Don't forget that after the snowstorm
> The fields again are visited by May.
> Don't forget your girlfriend,
> Who is your fate, your love.

In a word they enjoyed themselves and didn't start going home until after midnight, and Philharmon Ivanovich's father was at the celebration, too, although he recalled that at that time he was in hospital undergoing treatment for sciatica, and he said:

"It's good that we've all gotten together at least once in our lives. Everyone's here!"

Suddenly there was a laugh, and Philharmon Ivanovich went cold, expecting that it would be discovered that he had a boy living in his house on his stove.

"Who's that laughing?" asked his father.

"You only thought you heard it," said Philharmon Ivanovich.

"So what was I saying?" his father went on. "It's good, as I was saying, that every last one of us has come together today..."

And again the boy couldn't restrain himself and burst out laughing.

"There's someone laughing," said the elder Onushkin.

"It's wind in the chimney," said Philharmon Ivanovich.

A year went by and he said good-bye to the boy at the pond on whose dark surface floated white lilies and he asked:

"What were you laughing at when my father said that we'd all gathered together?"

"He didn't know," said the boy, smiling broadly, "that he'd soon come home and find his son had hanged himself."

Philharmon Ivanovich thought and remembered that his father had only one son and said:

"We've had a good year together. I don't want you to leave, and why are you so happy about it?"

"And I don't want to leave you," said the boy, putting his arms around him and holding him tight.

"I have no intention of taking my own life," said Philharmon Ivanovich.

"You know best," said the boy, growing sad.

Philharmon Ivanovich went back to his cottage and walked around to see if he were hanging anywhere, sat down at the window and started looking at the forest in whose shade the pond was hidden. For some reason the telephone started ringing sharply on the stove and he was forced to wake up with alarm in his heart.

It was eight o'clock in the morning.

"You just can't wait," said Philharmon Ivanovich to some-one or other and he remembered vaguely that someone in his family had hanged himself, a long time ago, from an unhappy love affair, he thought something like that had occurred, but who it had been he didn't have time to recall because the telephone had started ringing in an alarming way with exactly the same ring as on the stove in his dream.

It was one minute past eight.

From the very first words Philharmon Ivanovich realized that something was seriously wrong. The call came from the section which was located behind the door which was as solid as a safe, indeed the section was itself a safe. It was there that the most silent of all the silent people worked, the dullest of all the dull, those most privy to the biggest secrets of all secrets. If they ever rang anyone, it was almost always the beginning of their downfall, and if they rang them at home, especially two hours before the working day began and especially if the day before the secretary had banged the door shut, and especially if one's conscience were not crystal clear...

"But what's the problem?" Philharmon Ivanovich tried to ask, although he knew that it was useless, that he could never explain, they wouldn't care about your heart, they had no respect for age, because they were indifferent to you and your heart, age, cunning, kidneys, thoughts, feel-ings and other innards. He knew this but he still asked, the same way a fledgling probably can't help asking what the matter is when dragged out of its nest by a snake and swallowed down into the snake's cold insides. He asked and of course got no reply and no explanation and he was even more frightened because they didn't even hint at what the matter was.

Then two hours later he was sitting before an investigator who was asking him:

"Full name?"

"Philharmon Ivanovich Onushkin," he replied.

"Do you know an Ernst Zosimovich Biceps?"

"Yes..."

After work, where so far everything was as usual, except that the secretary of the section didn't greet him, he returned home and after thinking hard remembered that he had a patron and perhaps even a protector.

Several years before there had been a reception at the House of Friendship in honor of a delegation from a fraternal country — the same one, as a matter of fact, at which Philharmon Ivanovich's previous superior, a striking-looking, curly-haired, open-faced superior, had set out on his path from a bureaucratic career to selling strawberries. Philharmon Ivanovich and his wife were also at the reception. They ate hardly anything at all although orders had been given not to stand around like gate-posts during the *à la fourchette* occasion but to mix freely and animatedly in the spirit of the times. However, to stand on the sidelines, whatever the word from higher up was, was always less dangerous — you couldn't make any mistakes. The worst you could be accused of was having a private conversation, whereas for "making incorrect contacts"—Oi-Oi-Oi! Suddenly one of his own countrymen came up to him, a thin man of about sixty, and started to talk. He had the kind of appearance you don't easily forget — a long, hooked nose that almost touched his chin which stuck out like the pointed tip of a lady's shoe, while between his nose and his chin his lower lip jutted out and he had absolutely no upper lip at all. A lock of gray hair fell over his high forehead with its sunken temples, and the cheeks on his cheekbones were also sunken. His eyes burnt with an eternal fire, and in the fire there blazed kindness, sympathy and the weight of life's experience. His lower lids were tense and fixed and never relaxed for an instant.

"If something should happen," said his fellow country-man after chatting for a while about who each was, where he worked, whether he had been in the war or not and so on in this vein — and for a second a covering of love and friendship quenched the fire in his eyes — "if anything happens, out of the blue, you never know, things happen, ring me at home, don't feel awkward about it, I'll give you my number... You never know what might happen, anything could, as I know only too well..."

Philharmon Ivanovich didn't immediately believe his unexpected patron, and he waited for six months or so to see if there was something behind it but no, there wasn't, and then he hid away the bit of paper carefully on which was written comrade Taganrog's home telephone number. He hid it away and carried it around like a talisman, like a safe-conduct which everyone needs, literally everyone, and this bit of paper warmed his heart and he used to bring to mind his experienced friend's eyes, moist with kindness, and his telephone number.

"Yes," said the telephone receiver. "Who is it calling? Oh, Comrade Onushkin. How could I forget, my dear man, I remember the evening, and you, and your wife, who comes, as I remember, from the Irtysh River? From the Belaya? Business? Of course it's business, why else does anyone call me, heh-heh, my dear man, don't think about it twice, it was for a matter like this that I gave you my telephone number, wasn't it? I understand, I'll come to see you straight away, give me your address."

So comrade Taganrog was walking around Philharmon Ivanovich's apartment in person, saying:

"What a fine cat you've got! Peach? An original name,

I've rarely come across it among cats. Although I have come across it! Is there indeed anything in this world I haven't come across, you'll ask. If I wrote down the story of my life I'd get the Nobel Prize. I really would, yes, believe me, Philharmon Ivanovich, that's the truth. God knows. Do you believe in God? No, of course not, but I don't know, to be quite honest, but I suppose he probably doesn't exist, what do you say? Yes, well how's your health, how's your heart, not acting up? And how is your father? In the hospital? Fancy that...Well, never mind, perhaps they'll do him some good, although to be honest, there they've got the best conditions but the worst physicians,* isn't that so? Heh-heh, you're afraid. Don't be, you can tell me everything, you can and you must, Philharmon Ivanovich. So your wife has gone to visit her family? Nothing wrong with that, but it's time she came back, eh? You haven't got any children — perhaps you should see a doctor about it — I could find one for you. I've got more faith in folk medicine myself, the old, old women, a shame they suppress it, isn't it? Still, on the other hand, my dear friend, they rake the money in — thousands, tens of thousands, now I ask you, is that right?"

Philharmon Ivanovich took the vodka from the refrigerator and set it on the table, put out the snacks, sat his dear guest down and poured the drinks. Comrade Taganrog's soft voice radiated strength and tranquility. However, he declined a drink, saying that business came first. He got out a notebook and pen and told him to tell him his story in detail while he took notes in tiny writing. Philharmon Ivanovich told him everything — about Biceps, about his peculiarities, about the coat which he promptly showed his guest, about the seventy-three rubles, about going out vis-

---

Poly parketnye, a vrachi anketnye: This is a reference to the hospital for the elite where the equipment and conditions are superb but the medical staff is selected by political rather than medical criteria.

iting the night before and about the insistent manner of the investigator. And he begged for advice. Taganrog wrote everything down, rechecked the details, sat silently for a moment and then asked: "Have you told me everything?"

"Everything," said Philharmon Ivanovich, going over it all in his mind. The only thing he'd kept quiet about was his dreams, but he'd more or less mentioned everything else.

"Right, then," said Taganrog. "Tomorrow morning you must take the coat in to the investigator and hand it in, get them to sign for it. When you get to work, hand in your resignation on the grounds of personal circumstances. Then you must write it all down in detail and take it in to the proper authorities or send it in through me. You mustn't forget a single name and where you don't know a name give a physical description. And give your opinion of them, especially of the artistic director. Not everything's been lost yet, my dear man!"

"I don't want to," said Philharmon Ivanovich in a deep voice.

"Why are you speaking in that strange voice?" said comrade Taganrog, frowning.

"There's something wrong with my throat," Philharmon Ivanovich said in a frightened manner. "It seems my voice is suddenly changing..."

"Yes, everything moves on, everything changes," said Taganrog in a melancholy way. "You'll want to! There's no other way out of it, you'll want to!"

"I've got to find another way out, Comrade Taganrog," said Philharmon Ivanovich with a note of entreaty in his voice. "Let's have a drink and you think about it..."

"About what? It's been decided on at the highest level, yet you want to think?"

"The highest?"

"You don't believe me?" Taganrog became severe and distant. "Comrade Onushkin, although I'm only five minutes away from being pensioned off, I've still got friends, I assure you! I've got no time to have a drink. Look, if you don't want to write it, I'll have to."

They sat in silence. Philharmon Ivanovich looked stupidly at the floor. Taganrog got up and put away his notebook and pen with an air of determination.

"Comrade Taganrog," said Philharmon Ivanovich with some difficulty.

"Did I give you advice?" Taganrog asked severely. "I did. Was it correct advice? It was. Do you not want to take advantage of it? That's your business, Comrade Onushkin."

Philharmon Ivanovich also got up and unable to restrain himself looked comrade Taganrog in the eyes. His eyes had changed, they were empty of everything that had burnt in them before. Only the lower lids were the same as they had been, showing strain, while above them there was nothing — empty eye-sockets, holes like those in a skull.

And now, straight into these bold openings, where earlier understanding and benevolence had shone and not just black emptiness, in a way he could not have foreseen at all, Philharmon Ivanovich suddenly spat, like a boy from the village burning his boats and plunging into the Rubicon, now without any talisman...

Time, which passes quickly anyway, now raced forward at cosmic speed level two.

So Philharmon Ivanovich stood downcast before his immediate superior who had been recalled from the delights of his annual leave, listening to reproaches mixed with groans of pity — not for Philharmon Ivanovich, why pity him, but for himself, who because of this party official was innocently enduring great suffering:

"Things nearly got out of hand because of you, just

because of you! That wretched *Ichthyandros,* why did you have to mention it to outsiders, who put pressure on you? Fortunately I didn't read it, there are witnesses, I didn't read it! No, don't expect anything of me personally! Up there they could hardly wait for your benefactor to agree to take his pension and go. They celebrated for three days waiting for him to retire and then you had to come along! You couldn't have been expected to have seen through Biceps, although just off the record it's written all over this one in large letters!"

"Comrade Biceps...," Philharmon Ivanovich began but his superior plunged deeper into his personal grief and was unable to listen to his inferiors:

"Comrade! He made out he was a comrade! It was nothing less than some sort of hypnosis. He was just a non-Party nonentity, with a poor education, yet everyone knew him. He was everyone's friend and comrade, also a brother. The people he was involved with — hypnosis, that's all it was! He used to get into secret factories without a pass and meet generals from the capital in saunas! Comrade! It took them two years to uncover him and then it was only by accident. Who does he think he is, the upstart, not taking anything for himself, doing everything for others, the scoundrel, for others! Do you realize I could've been dismissed? Me? Anyway, there's nothing further to be said."

Later Philharmon Ivanovich stood before the investigator, on whose table lay a big parcel bound with ordinary string, and the investigator signed a docket to the effect that P.I. Onushkin was returning to the State a jacket which had been illegally obtained. And outside it was cold and the man in the tram and in the crowd looked odd — medium height, extremely well preserved, some might say stainless-steel in appearance, wearing a suit, a brown hat with the earflaps down and wrapped up in a scarf right up to and including his chin.

And then Philharmon Ivanovich was in a large room that had a white-marble bearded bust in the left corner and a different one in the right corner, although that was made of white marble too and also had a beard, and on the wall between the two corners there was an enormous portrait of Lenin in the process of striding forward. Under the portrait at a long, long table, right at the end, as if on a throne, towered the very top man himself, while on either side of the table sat the rest of the top men, the lower in rank, the more removed from the very top man, although not without certain justifiable exceptions. Others were not seated at the table but ranged on chairs along the wall — they did not raise their hands at the question "All those in favor?" In this room the manager of the secret enterprise had just become the former manager, although Biceps had in fact managed to get him the steel of the required kind, but they'd taken the steel and fired the manager, indeed they'd expelled him from the ranks of the Party for lack of vigilance, having contact with a scoundrel and a hundred other immoral acts. Other comrades had just revealed their mistakes, too, including the artistic director and the switchboard supervisor; however, in revealing them some had lost their jobs and party membership, some had just lost their jobs and some had gotten through unscathed for the time being. And then came the moment which had been set aside at this well-prepared meeting for the officer from the Cultural Section, Philharmon Ivanovich Onushkin, born 1919, member of the Party since 1945 and all the rest. He stood up when he heard his name, but first the comrade responsible for trade was asked to speak because the top man showed a humane interest in the problem of outer clothing for ordinary section heads and he reminded the meeting with some distaste, banging his fist on the table, that an order had gone out as early as August to get in supplies of sheepskin coats on the basis of distribution to everyone, right down to political officers. But the comrade responsible for trade explained that although they were delivered in August for the most part they were almost all distributed in August as well, on the instructions of people more responsible than he was, who was only responsible for trade. And here the top man frowned and looked at these more responsible people, and the more responsible people in their turn frowned and looked at a lot of other people, and these looked at all the rest and all the rest also frowned, and everyone looked at Philharmon Ivanovich who was standing there like a gatepost. Here the top man, thumping the table with his fist, with distaste ordered a new supply to be brought in and for it to be distributed on his, the top man's, written instructions alone, and not otherwise, and after this he ordered Philharmon Ivanovich to speak. And he began:

"Everything began with *Ichthyandros...*"

"Who?" the top man asked again.

"It's a poem in prose," Philharmon Ivanovich explained.

"What are you babbling about?" said the top man, banging his fist and looking around him, searching for someone with more sense.

Philharmon Ivanovich's immediate superior leapt up almost before the top man's glance touched him, and quickly said that the matter was quite clear, his behavior couldn't have been worse, his fall couldn't have been lower and he would move that he be swept out, purged. He still hadn't time to sit down when the head of among other things the investigatory organs stood up and said that that wasn't all, that Philharmon Ivanovich had also made out that he was some kind of simpleton and passed in his old overcoat to the investigator, deceitfully getting a docket for his sheepskin coat. However, under instruction and in conformity with the law, his old overcoat had been hung on his hook in the cloakroom while his sheepskin coat had been confiscated so that people could conclude for themselves that indeed the limit had been reached.

Then something happened which doubtless does not happen in such places or if it does happen, then only rarely and it shouldn't. Philharmon Ivanovich started taking off his coat, and undoing his tie. In short, he started getting undressed but so determinedly and unhurriedly that it would be more correct to say that he started to disrobe like a priest after a service, and as he did so he spoke quickly and incoherently:

"You can take the coat...I got my overcoat from the office supplies and my jacket too...take the lot...if I'd gotten it in August I'd still have paid seventy-three rubles...but I didn't get one in August, I wasn't even thinking about it in August...and you can take my tie... My shoelaces are my own but my shoes come from supplies... Take the lot, you wear them, don't feel troubled about it... Forty years I've worked, thirty-four in the Party, the war, the shirt's from supplies, too, I don't need it..."

"Get him out," said the top man with distaste. "Dismiss him and expel him from the Party. Unanimous decision."

And he added to his assistant over his left shoulder: "Find him another job till retirement."

Philharmon Ivanovich was taken out, dressed and then thrown out of the palace built in the style of Karl Ivanovich Rossi, this time for good.

When he got home, Philharmon Ivanovich gave Peach some milk to drink then picked him up and stroked him, saying:

"Why are you called Peach? You haven't got a single peach-colored hair..."

"That's what you called me, master," Peach answered.

"I called you! Well, you should change your name!"

"A dumb creature can't change its name," Peach objected.

"How can you be dumb if you're holding a conversation with me?"

"Well, that's what I'm doing, master, " Peach answered evasively.

"Don't call me master," Philharmon Ivanovich ordered him. "If someone addresses you as an equal, you are obliged to return the compliment. Always and everywhere!"

"You don't go everywhere," said Peach, obediently changing his tone.

"That's not something for you to poke your nose into!"

"Will you let me down, please?" Peach asked.

"All you cats are traitors — you rub up against our legs as long as you want something to eat but as soon as you've eaten your fill you couldn't care less about us," Philharmon Ivanovich said bitterly, putting the cat on the sofa.

"That's not quite so," Peach remarked evasively.

Then Philharmon Ivanovich gave evidence at Biceps' trial and heard his final words. Ernst Zosimovich spoke, as always, in an inexpressive voice but he took care that he was heard.

"Why did intelligent people, or seemingly so, trust so easily that I was invested with such enormous power," said Biceps, or words to that effect, "when I had no such power? I don't know, your Honor, you'll have to ask them, Duke forgive them.

"My view is that everyone needs something, there's always a shortage of friendship, even high level contacts. Why was it up to me to provide them with everything, each accord-

ing to his need? The prosecutor counted against me the
petrol, the drivers' labor, taking me and my friends around
town, and even the depreciation, but the point is that all
this was necessary in order to put me inside for longer, and
I didn't take a single ruble for myself! So why was it up to
me? Your Honor, I dreamt of becoming an actor and play-
ing Hamlet, Khlestakov, Tarelkin, all the best roles. It didn't
work out, I didn't become an actor. So I thought to myself,
why not see how Khlestakov would be received in real life?
He was received marvellously! All right, I'm prepared to
pay for my two years' triumph..."

"You besmirched what is most sacred in Soviet man —
the feeling of trust in one's neighbor!" the prosecutor interrupted him.

"Oh, 'tis sweet to hear the watch-dog's honest bark," said
Biceps sadly. "Duke forgive them. I won't go on about
Khlestakov, prosecutor. Don't forget, as you bring down the
sentence, that I am not a thief, or a spy, and I don't get
involved in politics, so that the most correct thing to do
would be to find me not guilty or give me a couple of years
on probation."

For embezzling state property (fuel, the chauffeur's
labor, depreciation on the cars) to an amount over ten
thousand rubles, for fraud and for hooliganism, Biceps was
sentenced to thirty years' imprisonment. After the trial outside on the street Philharmon Ivanovich thought he saw the
poetess Liza. She even appeared to be making her way
towards him, and he made off in the other direction as
quickly as he could, pulling his head down between his
shoulders. He would have pulled up his collar and hidden
his face if his overcoat had had the kind of collar you can
pull up in order to hide your face.

5. The Last Fact

Guided by surmises of a general nature, we might assume that the role of prisoner is not the one for comrade Biceps and that therefore he is bound to reemerge on the stage of life. The most likely thing is for him to turn up involved in foreign trade, for example, and to become famous for his successes, relying on his friendship with certain rulers, Greek shipping magnates, and Senator Edward Kennedy. Presumably he could only be completely done for through some accident, but then that can happen to anyone so that possibility will not be taken into account.

The day after the trial the telephone rang in Philharmon Ivanovich's apartment. Lately there had been one call he had feared, one which he waited for without having any idea of what he'd say, why should he have — it was easier like that — but all the same he kept waiting nervously. After a moment's hesitation he picked up the receiver. It was the doctor who was treating his father calling, and she said peremptorily that he would be discharged the next day and should be picked up at nine.

"What do you mean?" Philharmon Ivanovich asked. "The treatment isn't finished yet."

"It's the decision of the doctor in charge," said the doctor. "The only thing wrong with your father is old age and this is a hospital, not an old people's home!"

"Surely you can do something for him," said Philharmon Ivanovich, to which the doctor replied, lowering her voice, straight from the heart:

"What are you talking about? Who can we do anything for here?"

Obviously someone had gone out of the room she was ringing from, but then someone else, just as obviously, immediately came into the room because she then said in a loud voice: "At ten sharp, then."

And she hung up.

However, everything turned out differently from the way the doctor in charge had instructed. Philharmon Ivanovich's father found out about what had happened to his son because he was a mobile patient and that day comrade Taganrog was brought to the hospital. He was confined to bed and immediately called for Onushkin the elder and told him everything in confidence adding that he should write to someone "up there" and he, Taganrog, once he was well again, would give his assistance, which he could do inasmuch as he had intended retiring but he no longer intended to do so, and when he'd said all that he fell asleep, utterly exhausted. Onushkin immediately sat down to write and wrote in a state of excitement the whole day and the next morning he didn't wake up at the usual time, which caused no one any concern. He didn't wake up until Philharmon Ivanovich arrived and started to rouse him. His father took a moment to wake properly, looked at his son and recognized him. While they were sending for the doctor, who was having her morning five-minute tea break, the father looked at his son with recognition for half an hour and said nothing. Finally he swallowed, passed his tongue over his lips and said: "Please forgive me. Just forgive me."

After that he coughed briefly, let his head drop in an awkward way and fell silent. The doctor appeared, Philharmon Ivanovich was put outside in the corridor, from where a nurse called him into a ward where, as she put it, a friend was waiting to see him. Comrade Taganrog lifted himself up on one elbow with some difficulty and asked sympathetically:

"How's your father? Did he die?"

Philharmon Ivanovich was seized by a spasm from the hairs on top of his head which stood up on end to his toes which clenched themselves up, and then he did something which he expected least of all the unexpected things he'd said and done during those fatal days, and it was this: with two fingers he made the sign of the cross over Taganrog, after which the spasm passed.

"That's not new to me, either," said Taganrog, lying back on his pillow. "It never helped anyone, and won't help you, either."

As Philharmon Ivanovich was leaving, the cloakroom attendant came out from behind her counter and with unusual respect helped him on with his overcoat because the rumor about the visitor who made the sign of the cross in the hospital had already reached the junior staff.

To his regret, the baptized comrade Taganrog did not manage to give Philharmon Ivanovich the further aid he needed — he died towards evening, which was not surprising since almost everything that could be eaten away in his long-suffering body had been eaten by the disease whose name people fear as children fear the darkness.

Onushkin the elder's letter addressed "up there" turned out to have been addressed to the great leader who had passed away long ago so that after some consultation among themselves the doctors sent it on to someone else.

After that nothing really special happened. Only Philharmon Ivanovich attended his father's funeral, unless you count the driver and the grave diggers. Then he spent several days at home where, unless he was sleeping or dozing on his bed, he sat at the table reading his synopses. He read them as if he were looking for something he just couldn't find, putting to one side the notebooks he'd read and then taking them up again and skimming through them, hoping to light on something, so that he soon upset their variegated order. Now and again he seemed to find something. For instance, in the light-blue book with the number eighty-four on it, he reread several times, with noticeable thoughtfulness, the following: "As the idealist Marien-berger asserts, without ethics there are no aesthetics," but this was apparently not what he was looking for because he actually threw notebook number eighty-four on the floor. Then again he spent a long time thinking about the following words in the orange note book, number nineteen: "decisively sweeping aside the mystical fog which unites ethics and ontology in aesthetics," but even this notebook he put aside. So, not finding what he was seeking, he tied up his notebooks in parcels, with about ten in each, and took them away somewhere. No one ever saw these note-books again so that it's possible that he simply buried them somewhere.

Nobody knows what happened to Philharmon Ivanovich after that. Even in that place where, within the bounds of feasibility, records are kept of the careers of a great many people there is no clear information about him. According to certain sources he worked for a time as a guard at a store-house for coats, and then he started making fake Orenburg kerchiefs for the gypsies out of a yarn they had invented, a secret they don't give away to anyone, but which is probably cotton wool, with fiberglass and something else no one can quite make out. The gypsies apparently like him because he's so dumb and also because his productiv-ity is high, and apparently he has become very rich and through the gypsies has put his name down for a private car and exchanged his apartment in the city for a house with a garage in the suburbs. He certainly has changed apartments because when the telephone rang in his apart-ment the woman calling got a rude response, despite the fact that she spoke in a pleasant melodious voice; she was told that there was no one by that name living there and they didn't know where he'd moved.

According to other sources of information, Philharmon Ivanovich rejoined his wife in her village where they prac-tically live off the soil and make home brew from State sugar with the help of State water and State electricity and his wife has had a son by him whom they've called by the partly Russo-Bashkirian and partly Russo-Tartar name of Ruslan.

A third source has it that he learnt some extraordinary card tricks and travels around with them as part of a con-cert brigade, that he has been wildly successful and has formed a liaison with the brigade's female leader.

None of these reports has the ring of truth and none can be supported with documentary evidence, as a conse-quence of which a red question mark has been pencilled in the top left hand corner of each one.

Happily, Peach the cat has ended up with the poetess Liza — that is certain — and lives in luxury, and even his new-found passion for chocolates is being fully satisfied, a passion which is extremely rare in cats although cats are subject at times to the most improbable passions. Actually, it could be a totally different cat, just a namesake.

Unhappily, Philharmon Ivanovich's boss, who so humanely gave orders for him to be provided with another job, something he for some reason did not take up, was suddenly and without any reasons being given, appointed ambassador to New Zealand, which one of our touring companies visited shortly afterwards, and the former department head showed an unhealthy interest in one of the singers from his homeland, a lady with high breasts and long legs, and he even made a trip with her, and without a chauffeur, into the wilds of the New Zealand mountains, which the singer made a report about on her return, and the ambassador was recalled, dismissed, expelled from the ranks and made the deputy principal of some school that trains professional technicians, so that now high breasts and long legs, whoever they belong to, evoke in this naturally democratic man a smile of disgust. Everything does indeed flow on and change, although Philharmon Ivanovich is in no way to blame for these changes, and although a new head has quickly been found and appointed, it might seem as if nothing has changed—all the same the sheepskin coats which have recently arrived at the supplies section for the middle-range officials, including political officers, have again disappeared somewhere and no one can sort it out.

Unexpectedly, the poetess Liza no longer seeks anyone's protection, although she is offered it, and is writing a poem about the battle at Kulikovo for the six-hundredth anniversary of the occasion. The poem is called "Glimpses of Light" and even contains such lines as the following two:

They looked at each other in the mirrors of the shields
And instead of the enemy each saw his own likeness.

Her older friend told her that the shields in those times could hardly have served as mirrors and that she'd be better off writing prose and for the first time in her life the poetess Liza quarrelled with him once and for all.

However, one fact not recorded in these different reports so far is that Philharmon Ivanovich is seen at performances in different theaters. He now sits in the back rows, and just as before he likes everything that's put on to the point of oblivion, but in contrast to before he laughs, cries, suffers, whispers the actors' lines, prompting them, and claps with all his might, although how he gets into the theaters, and how he manages to disappear unnoticed after the show, no one has ever seen, which is not surprising because who cares about him?

An Absolutely Happy Village

To my wife Irina

1. The Beginning of This Song,

which is actually quite a lengthy one, is lost in the mists of time but it begins on the slope of the high bank of a dark blue river, near this forest, beneath this very sky. Our beloved czarina, Elizabeth, after abolishing the death penalty and thereby bringing forth the intellegentsia in our fatherland, commanded two Old Believers, Mikhei and Foma, to settle here. And so they settled here, hewed themselves cottages, acquired for themselves wives and children, and their children multiplied, their cottages also multiplied, their fields spread and their herds grew. Moving upon all this acquiring, multiplying, spreading and growing was history, according to its iron laws, so that the inhabitants first of all were serfs and had no land, then they became free, although they were no better off for land than before, then they became even freer and were given an abundance of land, after which they arrived at the apex of historical development where, on collective farms, they live to this very day. However, our subject is not history but, to start with, the cow.

A cow eats thistles with tender lips, and in her wisdom gives milk for the people.

A cow is like a village.

Her majesty the cow sat for centuries at the spinning-wheel, spent her life under arms from Poltava to Shipka, only the cow's crown is not on her head, but on her belly and is called an udder.

A village's crown is also on its belly.

From a city's chimneys there flows no milk, no meeting can give sour cream and there's nothing for a cow to eat on asphalt.

A cow feels sad, anyway, but all the more so on asphalt.

It is the highest praise to call a woman a cow, although not in our country, but in India. Because there men have an independent temperament.

"We've got our pennant on the moon, but there's no grass growing up there — it's the wrong sort of soil," Postanogov explained to his neighbor, as they sat thinking aloud about life on other planets.

"What you've got to realize is that there's nothing but virgin soil up there," his neighbor observed thoughtfully.

"And vast amounts of it," said Postanogov. "Everything is foreseen by the men at the top."

"As if I didn't know," thought his neighbor, out loud. "Now take the way they've let us keep a cow again. Whenever they forbid something, they always permit it again later, without fail."

"What I can't stand is someone carrying on about things," said Postanogov. "His eyes sticking out and his arms and legs quivering. More like a beetle than a man."

"You're calling me a beetle?" said his neighbor, taking offense, out loud.

"Who else?" asked Postanogov. "There are things that have to be thought about, but you keep on about 'the cow,' 'the cow'!"

"What is there to think about?" said his neighbor. "A cow's a cow and that's all there is to it!"

"Everything is foreseen by the men at the top," said Postanogov.

"That's not news to me," said his neighbor, offended again.

"Well, just stop carrying on about your cow!" said Postanogov.

"I haven't got a cow!" said his neighbor angrily. "I haven't had a cow for thirty years!"

"Do you know how much grain your cow would've eaten in thirty years?" said Postanogov. "What are we supposed to eat — grass? No, I don't like it when someone carries on about things and doesn't live according to a plan."

"What do you mean, not according to a plan?" asked his neighbor.

"It's obvious," said Postanogov. "What will you, for example, be doing in ten years' time?"

"That's impossible to say," said his neighbor.

"There you are, you haven't got a plan." Postanogov threw up his hands. "So what do you want a cow for?"

"What cow?" asked his neighbor.

"The one you haven't got," said Postanogov.

"I *don't* need the cow I haven't got," said his neighbor.

"So don't start getting smart," said Postanogov. "Live a peaceful life."

"There's nothing new about living a peaceful life for me," said his neighbor.

If anyone is wondering what the fundamental truth is about this historically formed village, it's right here in the words of Postanogov's neighbor, sitting quietly beside him on the bench beside the fence, his weather-beaten face, overgrown with a hard, gray stubble, turned towards the setting sun. It's an uncomplicated kind of truth, even rather paltry and essentially trifling, but all the same it's the fundamental truth, because the river flows, the earth turns green in spring, the rains pass unhurriedly over the fields, the people go unhurriedly to the fields, and the years pass unhurriedly through the village like the pilgrims who once wandered through the village to worship at holy places, not finding anything to worship here.

2. The Shoulder-Yoke

"Nothing unsettles me more than a shoulder-yoke," said Mikheyev. "It excites me so much I can't stand it. Well, of course there's nothing about a shoulder-yoke to excite any-one at all, and don't imagine there is, it's got an innocent shape and it's made of innocent material, but it excites me all the same. As soon as I see a shoulder-yoke, I feel like yelling for help. Only if you yell for help, when you're all excited, you look awfully silly.

"What I could do is explain that buckets are carried on shoulder-yokes, water is carried in the buckets, the water in the buckets is heavy, the yoke presses down on the shoul-ders, the shoulders are tensed up and then press down on the back, the back curves out and presses down on the behind, the behind sticks out and presses down on the legs, the legs straighten up, and the thighs tense up, and only women carry water in buckets on shoulder-yokes. And there aren't only old women in the village, but the occa-sional young one as well, especially in years past, when today's old women were young and, naturally, there were a lot more of them, I mean a lot more young ones, who are now old, because nowadays there are more old ones than young ones, that's why there used to be more young ones then than there are young ones now, and they used to carry water around on shoulder-yokes more, and their shoulders tensed up, their backs curved out, their behinds stuck out, their legs straightened up, but you can see what a long explanation we're ending up with and I'm still a long way from getting to the main point, which is what happens to me when I see a shoulder-yoke and know that on that shoulder-yoke they carry buckets and carry water in the buckets and the water in the buckets is heavy, and the yoke presses down on their shoulders and all those things happen that I could go into but won't, because I'd need a life-time to tell you about them all, there are so many details.

"The point of all this is that shoulder-yokes don't drive me crazy because the water in them is heavy and so on, but because they are often carried on shoulders and so on by, well, Polina, you know, the one whose dress and blouse I stole while she was bathing in the river and who I'll tell you about as soon as I can get rid of these shoulder-yokes. She dove in, and I jumped out of the bushes and grabbed her blouse and skirt and ran over to the willow and hid the blouse and skirt in the hollow of the tree and then sat down in the bushes again and she came out of the water and looked and looked and looked, and I couldn't help it and let out a snicker in the bushes, and she plopped straight back in the water, only that all came later — first of all I'll finish about the shoulder-yoke.

"She was walking along with the shoulder-yoke, and on the shoulder-yoke she had two buckets and in the buckets there was water and the water was heavy. I've already talked about that. She was walking along, and I was walking along two steps behind her, explaining to her, in an unhurried way, because there was no need to hurry, there was nowhere she could run off to with a shoulder-yoke and two buckets full of water, so I was explaining to her, in an unhurried way, how strong my love for her was and how strong our love for each other could be, and what strong children we'd have, and what remarkably strong grandchildren our children would have, and she kept trying to turn around to say something nasty to me or at least flash her eyes at me, but how could she turn around when she had that heavy shoulder-yoke across her neck so that she could scarcely turn her head. And, when she tried to turn all the way around, while she was still swinging around with her buckets, I had plenty of time to put on a bit of speed and swing around after her, so that however much she turned, I had plenty of time to turn around behind her curved-out back and say to her, go on, turn as much as you like, I like it because first of all, it means you're paying me attention, and the main thing, in the second place, is that you listen to me longer that way, and fill yourself up with love for me, which is why I took your skirt and blouse — I wasn't just up to mischief at all, I did it so I could talk to you longer because you never gave me the opportunity until I went out and hid your skirt and blouse in the hollow tree and then we had a proper talk because you had nowhere to go if you came out of the water, and you couldn't swim off and leave your skirt and blouse either, so there you were with your head sticking out of the water, looking at me, whether you liked it or not, and listening hard to what I said. Well, we turned around and turned around and then she walked on, because she had to carry the water and she couldn't keep turning around for too long. She was getting tired, so she kept walking, and she didn't have any luck trying to kick me either, because the water in the buckets was heavy and she had to keep her legs straight and you can't hop around on one leg like that, it doesn't matter how fit you are, so she just lashed out with one foot and then put it down again straight away, so as not to fall over altogether.

"So I kept following Polina around like that along the dusty road, and after the rain stopped as well, and now I can't look at a shoulder-yoke without getting excited. As soon as I look at one I feel as if my throat is on fire — first of all my mouth feels hot and dry and then my throat starts to burn and then my heart bursts into flame and then the whole lot of me is on fire. And I've become a danger to the village and harmful to the people, because I can't control myself when I see a shoulder-yoke and burst into flame. So, because of this shoulder-yoke, my life has become repulsive to me. Something must be done — I can't let it go on like this."

3. The River Polina Bathed in

The right bank sloped gently, as right banks are supposed to do, while the left bank sloped steeply and the sand martins burrowed into it, to build their nests — you could stick your arm into one of the holes up to your elbow and still not reach the nest, just as you can't reach out and touch the moon shining golden in the river in the evenings, when the sound of songs of an amorous nature carries across from the gardens, dark as a deep, still pond, and the river flows on busily, with no time to love the village more than she loves it already, no leisure to love it more, and I bathe in this river which hurries past, and she loves me coolly and tenderly, caresses my neck, my stomach and ankles, loving me to the extent I deserve, for I'm not big either when I'm in the river or in general.

And what is Mikheyev thinking? That I'm the most important thing in the world, so that he's unworthy of me and too limited for me, and he doesn't even want to go into the army until he's married me, although he's going to be called up soon and he'll have to go into the army, and I feel a bit sorry for him, but not to the point of tears, although my face is wet, but that's from the river.

I'm safely hidden from him now, and I've hidden my clothes, too, so that he can't find them, and I wonder where he's looking for me now, I wonder where he's rushing about looking for me.

"I'm here," I say, sullenly, from the bank, "where else? You hid from me safely, of course, and hid your clothes away safely, too, but you can't hide away from me, so here I am sitting on your clothes, waiting to talk to you about love, because I used to want to go into the army, to serve my time, but I don't want to at all now, and I'll dodge the call-up, even if they put me in prison, whatever they do to me, but I can't leave you, they'll have to shoot me first."

So what am I going to do with him? The river is no longer paying me the attention it should, and I feel so sorry for him I could cry, even if he is unworthy, because they're going to shoot him, and I'm getting so furious I could shoot him myself this minute. I can't bear it, and I'm leaving the river, and I wish you'd drop dead, you wretch, go on, go and hang yourself.

"Polina," I say to her, "please try to understand me."

"How can I understand you!" I say and start crying, and I'm shaking with all my sobbing and fury, and I huddle up against him so as not to tremble.

The river runs on, swishing and babbling, without raising her eyes to look at us, and I embrace him and I embrace her and I whisper something to her and I sob something to him in a whisper, and oh! that Mikheyev! and oh! that Polina! and oh! that river!

4. Out in the Field in the Hot Sun

The women were out in the field weeding, deployed in a long line, and the oldest of them, Fima, was out in front like Chapayev leading his men, except that she didn't have a sabre in her hand, but a chopper. And when you weed, you have to be able to bend over, but with ease, without hunching yourself up, so that you can breathe deeply, wholeheartedly while bent double, even though your stomach is folded in two and presses up against your chest and stops you taking deep breaths. The choppers were falling and rising, falling and rising, not in unison but haphazardly, and only sometimes, by coincidence, did it happen that they fell and rose with one stroke, and then they were falling haphazardly again.

Meanwhile, the men were standing around the combine tractor, discussing why it wouldn't go, except for the tractor driver who had buried himself in the engine, with only the soles of his feet sticking out.

And the sun was mercilessly baking the potato field, the dusty road, the engine which smelt of iron and grease, the yellow wheat field, the village off in the distance and the beads of sweat on the brigade leader's nose.

"He's not going to get it going," said the brigade leader intently. "Let's give it another push, eh?"

"We've already pushed it," said one-eyed Fomin.

"We could give it another push," said the other Fomin.

The women finished the row, straightened themselves up, wiped their faces, set up a babble for a moment, then veered round in a circle, bent over again and started back in a line, that is to say forwards, but in the opposite direction.

5. The Scarecrow in the Garden

The moon was shining under the peak of his cap into his primeval eyes, while all around him the sunflowers waved their black heads.

At home somewhere nearby, a cow lowed sleepily, a fish splashed in the river, and the ripples floated on the water, at the speed of the current.

"Have you been with Polina?" asked the scarecrow.

"Yes," said Mikheyev. "She doesn't want to marry me. She's being stubborn. She says, all right, so I love you. What else do you want, you good-for-nothing? Getting married to you would be too much. You'd get the idea you had complete power over me, and I couldn't stand that. I'd hang myself. So I said, what do you mean, complete power over you, when I love you so much? And she said, that's just what I mean. What will be left of me, if I not only love you but am also your wife? There'll be nothing left. I said to her, everyone does it, everyone gets married, there's nothing wrong with it, nothing to be afraid of, and we can't keep going like this, working all day and talking at night. But she said, well, we don't have to talk, so I said, how are we going to come to any decision if we don't talk, and she said, there's nothing for me to come to any decision about with you. What do you mean nothing, I said, when we have to come to a decision about getting married. No, she said, there's no need to come to a decision about that at all, because you'll only snore and I'll be miserable with you sleeping and me not sleeping. Then you sleep too, I said. There you are, she said, you're already trying to get complete power over me — you're sleeping so I've got to sleep too, well I mightn't want to. Well, I said, I won't sleep either. So why get married, she said, what difference would there

be, she said, if we don't sleep as it is and wouldn't sleep
then either. But, I said, we can't go on like this, working all
day and talking at night. But she said, if we can't keep going
the way we are now, then we couldn't keep going then
either, what's the point of getting married if we can't keep
going like this anyhow. So I said, everyone gets married and
keeps going, and she said, you've got yourself in a complete
muddle and haven't got any idea what you're saying, and I
said, I have not got myself in a muddle, I said, everyone gets
married and keeps going, so we would too, and she said,
they probably stop loving each other and I couldn't stand it
if you stopped loving me, I'd hang myself. What are you
talking about, I said, I'll never stop loving you, because
you're the best there is and I don't want anyone else but
you. No, she said, you're just saying that to talk me round,
but once you've talked me round then you'll be saying
something different. I'll never say anything, I said, and she
said aha! so you won't say anything, you'll just keep quiet,
and if you're going to keep quiet, that means you'll go to
sleep, but I won't and I'll be miserable and I'm not going to
marry you. Well, we talked like this all night, spinning
round and round on the spot — marry me, I won't marry
you, become my wife, I won't become your wife, but we
can't keep going like this, we won't keep going anyway,
everyone gets married, but you said I was better than everyone else, but even the very best get married, so what, I don't
want to. She was being stubborn. And where are we going
to meet, when winter comes? Wherever you like, she said. I
want to meet somewhere warm, I said. Why aren't you a
normal woman, everyone wants to get married, but you
don't want to. I have no idea, she said, who'd want to marry
you, I just can't imagine such a fool, except perhaps some
madwoman. No, I said, completely normal women do. Well,
she said, go and marry your normal women, if I'm not

normal. No, I said, what do you mean, it's only in this one thing that you're not normal, in everything else you're better than the most normal of all. How am I better than all the others, she said, what are you going on about that for, I'd like to know. So I said, it's very hard to explain to you, because I don't know the words, I'm not very educated. Then go and educate yourself, she said, what would I want with an uneducated husband? Well, we talked on and on like this, all night. We even got quite weary.

"I'd be interested to know, too," said the scarecrow, "how exactly is she better than all the others?"

"That's what's got me thinking," said Mikheyev. "I haven't gone to bed, even though every bone in my body is groaning, wanting to go to sleep, but instead of going to bed, I'm standing here with you, thinking aloud, because tomorrow night I really must explain it to her — she really wants to know, I can explain it to myself, but I can't put it into words, so I say just marry me and she says, no I won't, but you know the rest, I've already told you.

"You're standing still," said the scarecrow, "just like me."

"I'm not bored, though," Mikheyev objected.

"Of course you're not," said the scarecrow. "A fool is bored standing still, but no one intelligent ever is."

"But I'm not standing still, anyway," said Mikheyev. "Yesterday, we went across the river, and today we were over in the sunflower patch, but what's going to happen when winter comes? At home I've got my aunts, and although they're not all that old, they're light sleepers, and she's got her mother at her place, so where will we be able to sneak off to, in winter? Besides, even in the fall, there's rain."

"Come into the barn with me," said the scarecrow. "You could clear a space behind the sacks there. It would be like in a bomb-shelter, you could make yourselves comfortable there."

"She'd be embarrassed with you there," said Mikheyev. "She's always embarrassed about something or other, and you keep too much of an eye on things."

"I'll be asleep," said the scarecrow, "I'm fast asleep from the fall to the spring."

"Do you have dreams?" asked Mikheyev.

"Yes, I do," said the scarecrow. "I have very interesting ones. I'll tell you about them sometime, but now you should go off and have your own dreams, because the cocks will be crowing soon and the birds will wake up and I'll have to watch the garden."

6. The Hoary Old Man Hears the Earth Rumbling

The author has just been telling you about this, to his benign view, absolutely happy village without informing you, so far, either of where precisely it is situated, or what it looks like, as a whole.

As far as where exactly it is situated is concerned, this is something the author is not going to tell you. Not for anything. In Russia — and that's as far as he'll go. He'd die before he'd tell you anything more precise than that. He's got his reasons for this. And the first of these reasons is that he doesn't want to make it possible for others to check him out. This is, after all, a terribly bad period for people with a vivid imagination. Not that any such idea ever entered the author's head, — why should anyone arrest or not arrest him? That would be awful...

Without any allusion to politics, the author declares that it is a rotten period for people with a vivid imagination, and not at all because they might put you in jail, — it's simply a lousy period for people with a vivid imagination. Because everyone wants to check everything out, in every detail... They'll stick their nose in, check up on the author — whether or not he's portrayed everything precisely as it is, letter for letter, full stop for full stop, and the author will find this unpleasant, because he'll be forced to tell them unpleasant things, things they'll take offense at, and to try to convince them that in nature there can be no village which is the same for them and for the author — only my village exists, while theirs doesn't. And it is stupid to check me out, but they're not idiots either, and they'll think it over and come up with something I'll find offensive, for example, that I write exactly like Francesco Machado. "And who's he?" I'll ask in bewilderment, and at that point in our polemic, I would suffer irreversible defeat as I'd reveal, apart from my lack of originality, ignorance as well, unforgivable in a Russian, because a Russian patriot should know Francesco Machado — otherwise, as far as many people are concerned, he's not a patriot but a chauvinist. Just try to prove to them then that personally you have nothing against this Francesco person and would be delighted to acquaint yourself with his works, but that at the moment you have other things on your mind, at the moment you're concerned about this village. Aha! they'll say, you're interested in your own people, but not interested in other peoples, is that it? You're concerned about your own village, but don't give a damn about all the other villages in the world? And so because of Francesco, you'll end up being a chauvinist and as a chauvinist you'll be finished, and it's all because you're concerned about this village of yours. Why should the author suffer this irreversible defeat in a polemic? He won't say where his village is and that's all there is to that!

As far as what it looks like as a whole, this is something

he can tell you about with pleasure. Imagine a blue, blue
river, with a high, hilly left bank, full of ravines, and on this
bank a village spread out under a blue, blue sky. Well, if you
were to take a boat and row down the blue, blue river to the
edge of the village and look at it from there, you'd see there
on the outskirts an uncommon-looking house — not even
exactly a house, in fact, but a sort of astounding structure
that arrests the gaze straight away as soon as you start looking at the village. This structure was hewn from logs about
three meters long. In one wall a door was sawn out, in
another there was a small opening which was later boarded
up and stuffed with old rags. The roof of the structure
started to give way and kept giving way until it gave right
away and was left in an inviolable state for the rest of eternity. It was covered with the earth which washed across it,
and in this earth mosses, grasses, flowers and a small birch
took root. This strange dwelling has sunk down into the
sandy soil right up to its window so that now only six layers
of beams stick out of the high grass. No one in the world
can remember when this house first appeared here,
although it was already on this very spot when Russia was
invaded by the Napoleonic hordes.

From time immemorial, the hoary old man had lived in
this log hut, living as if at a remove from life at large, on the
outskirts, for some unknown reason uninvolved in anything, probably from old age, although he was perfectly
able to get about, never knew an illness, had black eyes,
plenty of teeth, and he didn't even wheeze when he was
digging potatoes in his little garden. But he never got
involved, — he bought bread, salt and matches once a
month at the store, without engaging in conversation.

On this evening, soon after the sun had set and the sky,
tinged with green in anticipation of the moon, was rising
higher and higher over the village so as to be higher than

the stars and to unveil them, Polina left the house and set
off to see the hoary old man, carrying some presents in a
little bundle. She walked in her bare feet across the gentle
earth and the even gentler grass, and she walked lost in
thought, for all to see — indeed, there'd have been no point
in trying to conceal herself because it was not yet dark.

It was the middle of June, that particular, wonderful middle of that particular June, which was later to deceive the
inhabitants of the village so extraordinarily, rumbling over
their heads in a historic storm, senseless from the point of
view of the gentle grass, the blue, blue river and the window all boarded up and stuffed up with rags. And for a
long, long time afterwards, learned men tried to fathom the
causes and the consequences, argued and even exchanged
insults, disagreeing about who was to blame, why such a
disaster had happened at all and trying to think up a way
to make sure nothing like it ever happened again. But this
was all much later, and now Polina was walking in her bare
feet to see the hoary old man and the first star had risen
beneath the sky, and the sound of frogs croaking was coming up from the river, and in a barn beside the road a cow
mooed vacantly. It was almost like a yawn, she just mooed,
she gave a totally meaningless moo, although a harmless
one, and old Yegorovna, the cow's owner, who was dozing
lightly at the time, started up with a thudding heart,
remembered all about the cow and realized that the cow
had simply been mooing, for no reason, because it had
eaten and drunk its fill, and Yegorovna's fingers remembered the slippery udder, and her eyes remembered the
crimson drop of blood which came out of the bursting
udder with the white milk, and Yegorovna strained the milk
twice, and there were lots of other things to do as well —
there were the onions to pick for sale, and her three grand-
daughters and Granddad Yegor to feed, and the eldest to

give a good talking to, so she wouldn't stay out too late having a good time, she wasn't big enough yet. And when she gave a start at the mooing, Yegorovna remembered all this, but she couldn't settle down and go to sleep again and that's why she also remembered her son and his bride and how fifteen years ago they had left her and gone their own way and begun to accumulate their own possessions and then these possessions had been taken away from them and her Andrei and Klava had been sent to live far away, where nothing grew and they had sent their daughters back to her, and at first they had written, and then they'd stopped, and old Yegorovna had wept over their letters — she used to start almost as soon as she'd seen the postman, and then, over and over again as she read and re-read the letters, but now there was nothing to cry over, tears no longer flowed over the old letters.

Polina was walking across the gentle grass, which was already dewy, and the moon bathed her, and the whole village, and the hoary old man's dwelling in light.

The old man was lying on a bench, hoarily and timelessly, with his ear to the wall, listening to the distant rumblings of the earth. The earth told him of the footsteps approaching his house; he sat up on the bench, lit the kerosene lamp and began watching the door, his hands on his knees.

In his clear head, simple thoughts lived simply and easily, like the roots of trees, not at all tangled because there's nothing tangled about roots. Only an ignorant man gets tangled up in roots, the tree doesn't get tangled up in them, the tree's not fool enough to go getting tangled up. It knows what it's doing when it puts down its roots, just as deep as is necessary and as wide as is needed, and the old man's needs were as wide as our whole planet and as deep as God Himself, in Whom, however, he had long ago completely stopped believing, because he had not been able to feel Him out, so that he went as deep as — but no further.

Polina knocked on the door and, bending down, went in.

Andrei and Klava were sent far away to live where nothing grew and they sent their daughters back from there. At first they wrote and then they stopped, but they kept on living there, although all around nothing grew, but man clings onto life, unless he loses heart. All around them were people they couldn't understand, although they weren't unkind. When they spoke they used words like megedbabarmodyery, although they weren't unkind. Andrei and Klava must not be forgotten, even though they'll never see their absolutely happy village again, nor their daughters Faith, Hope and Charity; little Faith is the eldest, fourteen years old.

"I need your advice, old man," said Polina, putting her presents on the table, and the old man looked at them, and through the kerchief the presents had been tied up in, he could tell, in his wisdom, what they all were — the eggs, the bread, the bottle of milk and the honeycomb — and he realized that the advice being asked of him was serious. He looked at Polina through her guileless clothes and thought about her, in his straight-forward way, grasped all her seriousness and said: "I listen to the earth, my child. The earth has been rumbling for a whole month now, do you understand?"

Far from the absolutely happy village, near the town of Magdeburg, a man named Franz, at this very moment, left a brick house with a red-tile roof, and his fair-haired wife and fair-haired children went with him, past other neat houses, past a neat silo, past squares of beautifully tilled earth to the train, and put him on the train and he went away. He must also be kept in mind, because he is directly linked to the old man's conversation with Polina, or, to put it more exactly, to the consequences of this direct conversation.

"I don't understand," said Polina. "Listen to me, old man, I need advice, and at the moment, I couldn't care less whether the earth is rumbling or not."

The old man smiled at her unawareness and dullness, the warm stupidity of a body still too young, and said: "I've already told you everything, child, saying that the earth is rumbling. That's what you most need to care about right now, in your condition."

"You're an old man," said Polina, getting angry. "Have you forgotten how to listen or something?"

"No, I haven't forgotten," said the old man and got ready to listen to what he already knew.

"Well, listen to what I've got to say and don't interrupt," said Polina. "I'm pregnant, and Mikheyev's pleased about it. He says now you can't help being my wife, but I don't want to be and I don't want to have the baby. Help me, old man, I can't get rid of it; can't you tell me some herb or other, you know everything. Mikheyev just laughs and says no such herb exists which could turn out to be stronger than me and my love and its outcome, because my love for you is strong and I'm strong and you're strong and our children will be strong and this is only the start, the first one. And I say to him, I love you, too, but I'm not going to marry you, you want to get complete power over me and I don't want to have this first one, he'll take after you, and you and I are enough as we are, what do I want with another one. And he says, not just one, there'll be a whole heap of them and more, and I say, you've gone off your head, what do I want with all those little Mikheyevs, and he says, that's what you say now, but afterwards you'll talk differently, we'll have ten of them at the very least, because we're young, you and I, and all ten of them will be very handsome, boys every one of them and Mikheyevs every one of them, real little fighters, can't you just see them? Yes, I can, I say, and it makes me feel sick. You feel sick from being pregnant, he says, but later you'll feel fine, and you can't have a baby without a husband, your mother would get upset, and you're her only daughter, she brought you up without a father, and she could get sick if she got upset, or even something much worse, and nothing will come of trying to get rid of it, there's no potion on earth could help you after we made love the way we did. So tell me the potion, old man, you've seen everything, and know every-thing—you even saw Napoleon, so they say, surely you can help me?"

"I did see Napoleon," said the old man. "I was still a boy, and he rode on a black horse — terrifying, enormous, with a cannon in his hands. It was a long time ago, my child."

"In films he's small," said Polina.

"That's only if you're looking at him from a distance," said the old man. "But I saw him from close up, as close as you are. He was a terrible man. You mustn't try to get rid of it; the earth has been rumbling for a whole month already."

"What's that to me?" asked Polina. "Your earth is rum-bling, so I have to have a baby because of this Mikheyev and become Mikheyev's wife, is that it?"

"What a dullard you are," said the old man. "You can't think things out, can you? Why do you think my ear hears the earth rumbling, down there? There are trains on the move. There's a lot of rumbling so that means there are a lot of heavy trains on the move. They're moving in one direction, notice. Don't you read the papers? Haven't you heard about the Germans? I know the Germans, I've seen them the way I can see you. There are trains on the move, which means they're carrying troops, which means there's going to be a war, which means they'll take your Mikheyev off to fight, which means he might get killed and you'll be left without any Mikheyev at all, unless you have this baby you're carrying. Do you understand now why you shouldn't be thinking about a potion, when the earth is rumbling? Have you done yourself much damage?"

"No," said Polina.

"What did you try?" asked the old man.

"As if you didn't know," said Polina. "Spurwort, lime-blossom, juniper...."

"That's nothing," said the old man. "Like water off a duck's back to a baby."

"Why did you say he might get killed, old man?" asked Polina. "You don't mean for sure, do you?"

"No, not for sure," said the old man. "It's possible, though. But you're going to give birth to a new Mikheyev."

"Tell me, how did he manage to win out over me?" asked Polina. "I have to love him, and I have to marry him, and I have to give birth to his first child, and I have to be sick at heart for him, and I cry for him, the rotter, whenever I think that he'll get killed. Why is it, old man, why do I cry?"

"That's something no one can know," said the old man. "However, that's what happens."

"Does it ever not turn out like that?" asked Polina.

"Yes, it does," said the old man.

"Perhaps you've made a mistake about it all, old man?" asked Polina. "About both the war and the trains? Perhaps I'd be better off doing what I've been doing and not giving it another thought?"

"No," said the old man. "I haven't made a mistake. You must give it thought. The railway line runs near us, I can't have made a mistake. And I read the paper. So that I can penetrate to the very center of what's going on. And, at the very center of what's going on, everything's as clear as day, there's nothing complicated about it there."

"You can see it all, but no one apart from you can see it?" asked Polina.

"They see, but they don't notice," said the old man. "It's easier for them not to notice. They look around the edges and miss the main thing. It's from youth and a lack of understanding."

"I'll go," sighed Polina. "He's waiting for me, the wretch."

"...I never thought," thought Mikheyev, "that she could sometimes be so submissive and obedient, without any fresh reasons to be. When, for example, I embrace her and she cuddles without saying a word, or when I ask her if she's going to have our first child, and she cuddles up even more; I ask if she'll marry me, and she cuddles up even more and nods her head into my shoulder, in affirmation, but I can't understand why one of her tears rolls down my skin."

"Why are you crying?" Mikheyev asked me.

"I don't want you to get killed," I said.

7. The Well with Bucket and Pole

I'm the well with bucket and pole and the only time I get any rest is at night. In the day-time I have to squeak and rattle, bend over and straighten up again, and listen to women's gossip. Lots of people think I can see the stars, but it's not so, I can only see the stars at night, when everyone can see them, but in the daytime, I get all the women's gossip so that I know everyone in the village, even before they're born, and all the more so afterwards. And I also know about everything that goes on in the world. I'm not like that garden scarecrow no one except Mikheyev talks to over there, past the poplar, the one he talks to at night, as if that scarecrow could know or understand anything, its simply that Mikheyev's passing by. He ought to talk to me, I could tell him things about himself even he doesn't know or simply half-forgets. He lives, for instance, with two hard-working aunts who, being unmarried, brought him up till he came of age, and he can hardly be expected to remember his father and mother, since they died before he learned how to remember. His two jolly aunts cheerfully reared him and loved him like a son, because all the sisters once loved his father, all at the same time, but it was only the youngest who got him all to herself, fur cap and great-coat over his shoulder and all, his forelock hanging down to his dashing eyebrow, a good-humored, educated man, but quarrelsome and a terrible trouble-maker. He made trouble with everyone, although he knew how to work, too. My women say when they're gossiping that it wasn't only the youngest who got him, but that there was enough of him to go round all the sisters, but I think they say that just in case, so that if anything had happened they wouldn't be left looking foolish, — women don't like being left looking foolish, that's why they provide for every eventuality, that's the reason they never make a mistake in anyone's favor, always the opposite, they'll never make anything out to be better than it is, and doubtless that's why I have such an untrusting and even sceptical nature, because the women keep providing for the worst eventualities and don't provide for the better ones. And this is what's called gossiping, and a sceptic is a gossip in the same way inasmuch as he doesn't make provision for the good side of things, either, except that he doesn't descend to details, and I don't think there's anything bad about that, so long as life goes along normally, but as soon as it doesn't then it's worse than the grinning skull buried next to my shaft, which was buried deep in the earth long before I was dug. Take the stars, which I swear I can't in fact see in the daytime, and a sceptic will say that there's nothing much on them, or moss and lichen at most, and gray-colored at that, and that's all there is in the whole universe, moss and lichen, and even that's unlikely, however far you fly at the speed of light in any direction. And that's more frightening than the skull, which once was a head, possibly a Tartar's, or some Russian warrior's, or perhaps no one knows whose it was, because only we here on earth have green grass and trees, white snowdrops in spring and red poppies in summer, and only here can you peer at the pattern on a butterfly's wing, on the leaf of a poplar tree, on a stump or on someone's face, and the whole of the universe with its gray mosses and lichens, it turns out, depends on this butterfly's wing, which city folk so admire, or on our absolutely happy village, which is one and the same thing, and it's so sad that the water in me might almost not be spring-water but pure tears, if the sceptics about the stars were right. But they're mistaken and for the worse, just like the women about the sisters, in my opinion, when they claim that they shared Mikheyev the elder, which is not true. The first two loved him but it was only the third one who possessed him, body and soul, although he was, of course, a red-blooded male with an appropriate breadth of frivolousness, but his son was broad in quite a different sense, and he set the wedding celebration for the Saturday, after he and Polina had first registered their marriage. She had agreed to this but she wouldn't agree to a wedding-feast for anything — they stood beside me for a long time arguing about it, with each other.

"What sort of wedding-feast would it be if I'm giving birth in five months?" said Polina.

"But how can we not have a wedding-feast," said Mikheyev, "then every year for the rest of our lives we'll remember that on this very day we didn't have a wedding-feast and feel more and more bitter every year, and we've got a lot of years to live, and over all those years we'll work up a lot of bitterness. And why should we — our first-born will resent us for being so stupid on his account and not going through with the wedding-feast, though you wouldn't even know he's there yet, still every year he'll get cleverer and cleverer and we'll seem to him more and more stupid for having refused to have a wedding-feast over such a trifle."

"But what sort of wedding-feast would it be if I feel awkward about wearing a white dress?" said Polina.

"Don't wear a white dress, then," said Mikheyev, "or wear it with, well, for example, a red sash, because it's no one else's business that we're already lovers and that you wouldn't agree to marry me before — that's your deeply personal business — and just let anyone try to say something, or even give you so much as a look, I don't care if it is a wedding-feast, I'll soon give him something to look at, so he doesn't stick his nose in your business. He's got enough business of his own to look after, let him look at himself if he wants to look at something. If he looks at you I'll show him, I'll show him every year on that day, there'll be blood and teeth everywhere, I'll chase him clear out of the village, but I'll find him on that day, wherever he is, he needn't think I won't, so don't be afraid, you wear what you like."

"But what sort of wedding-feast would it be if you're going to do all those terrible things?" said Polina. "What do I want with a party where you're going to bash up the guests and perhaps even my relatives the way you say you're going to?"

"Not only yours but mine, too," said Mikheyev. "I won't favor anyone, but I'm sure it won't get to that because in the first place everyone loves you and in the second place, everyone knows me, the same way they knew my father and the same way everyone will know our first-born, so we're not going to let you be insulted. Don't worry, wear whatever you like, even an old gossip like Grandma Fima loves and cares for you — we can go through with the wedding-feast without any worries."

I smiled when he mentioned Grandma Fima, a small, dried-up old woman, but with a voice like the archangel Gabriel's, because, although Mikheyev didn't know it, it was she and no one else who was so mistaken for the worse about his aunts. There's just one conversation I remember between Mikheyev's mother and the eldest of the sisters, a long, long time ago. They stood right here on the spot these young ones are standing on. It was a short conversation but not really to the point, and no one heard it except me, which is just as well, or else Grandma Fima would have drawn conclusions from the vagueness to her advantage, in the worst possible sense. This is how the conversation went:

"Leave me be!" said the youngest sister.

"Take them, please, I want you to," said the eldest.

"Leave me alone!" said the youngest.

"I can't wear them anyway, people will talk," said the eldest.

"What do I care?" said the youngest.

"Then I'll simply throw them out; I've got a good mind to throw them down this well," threatened the eldest.

"Go right ahead!" said the youngest. "Or else give them to me and I'll do it."

And she did. And they're still lying in me, those beads of real pearl, and how Mikheyev's father came by them, during the stormy years of the civil war — by force, or as a present, or whether he picked them up by chance somewhere — they don't say, because they choked when they sank and got stuck deep down inside me, caught on the sides. And if anyone should ever find them and bring them back up into the light of day, what an interesting tale they could tell. Why he gave them to the eldest sister will never be clear, and why should anyone need to stir up the past, such as it is, and drag it up into the light, the light of day, out of wells and other dark corners, and disturb the dead, who didn't even enjoy being alive and don't enjoy sleeping in the damp earth — it would depress the cheeriest, happiest man, that would, sniffing out all sorts of nasty things about him, and trying to find out things about his father and mother and whether or not they were hiding anything, and disturbing his two grandfathers and two grandmothers, and his four great-grandfathers and four great-grandmothers, and you'd pile up such a collection of disgraceful things over, let's say, twelve generations of his personal relatives, taken only in the most direct line. He'd have two thousand and forty-eight great-great and so on, ten times over, grandmothers, and no less than two million plus ninety-seven thousand plus one hundred and fifty-two great-great and so on, twenty times over, grandmothers, and exactly the same number of great-great and so on, twenty times over, grandfathers, and every single one of them, well, almost every single one of them, with negligible exceptions for such a number, would no doubt have sinned in some way or other, which is something he wouldn't be very keen to talk about, what he'd be keen about would be for it to lie buried with him in the damp, forgetful earth. For that matter, such a mountainous pile of disgraceful things would be a burden for his progeny, too, if only he knew about it: it would be enough to crush you. It's no joke — it would take an enormous amount of time to work your way through such a huge number of people and make some appropriate judgment on each one of them, to form a just

opinion about each of them, conscientiously, and give each
his deserts. It would be an impossible labor for anyone —
life is not long enough for all one's own relatives, let alone
other people's, and a person has still to live his own life and
everyone wants to do that, wants to live according to his
conscience, honestly, so as to be numbered among the few
exceptions and not in the boring ranks of great-
grandmothers and great-grandfathers, even if he doesn't
want it constantly but only sometimes, when he doesn't
happen to want anything else but does possess this noble
desire, when he doesn't possess any other desire, but pos-
sesses this in all its tempting lustre, so that he simply has no
time for great-grandfathers. It's all the more true now, at
this particular time, this is something that I, being the well
with bucket and pole, and having both a certain profundity
and an outlook, know for certain because once our school
teacher, Fyodor Mikhailovich Shtanko, was reading a book
and I took a look at it and read in it the following, literally:
"This is because the time has come to save our land for
ourselves, because our land is being ruined not from the
invasion of twenty foreign tribes, but by us ourselves."
Where he got such a seditious book I don't know, nor do I
know what it was called, because the book was covered by a
page of *Pioneer Truth.** It was easy to read the name of the
newspaper, but not the book, and Fyodor Mikhailovich sat
there for a long time thinking, his arms around his knees,
looking out over the river and the wood, thinking, probably, about how to save our land, and what I don't know is
whether he thought up anything, but even without any
effort on his part, he was a very good man and not because
he was very old, he was very good before that, in his youth.
He taught all the children at the school. At Mikheyev and
Polina's wedding he made a speech, a speech completely

Pionerskaya pravda: a children's newspaper published in Moscow.

appropriate to the occasion, nothing about saving anything in it, I imagine, because it would have been out of place to talk about such things at a wedding; he just recalled the newlyweds' good points from their school days and encouraged them to turn to him for advice or help, if they ever needed it and not to be embarrassed about it. Actually, Fyodor Mikhailovich's speech was the last intelligible speech that was made. After that everyone at the wedding let their hair down and there was complete disorder. The women laughed kittenishly "aahhaha!, aahhaha!" while the men laughed in dogs' voices "hohoho!, hohoho!" In a word, after that people enjoyed themselves however they pleased, talked to whoever they pleased about whatever they pleased. The women did a lot of gossiping, standing around me early the next day, but despite this, I didn't manage, all the same, in the space of that morning, to put together a clear picture of what happened and later, from about twelve o'clock onwards, or possibly even a little earlier, no one talked about the wedding any more, they had other things on their minds. I couldn't see the wedding very well, because of the apple orchard and the elder bushes beyond which stands the house Mikheyev and his cheery aunts live in, and I couldn't hear very well because of the noise, so the only people I could see well were the guests who came around this side of the bushes, but it was impossible to come to any interesting conclusions from what they did on this side of the bushes. So I can only tell you the trivial details I heard from the women. Grandma Fima, in particular, reported that when the guests cried out "Kiss!", the first time, Mikheyev answered "Kiss yourselves, why don't you," but then Polina put her arms around him and kissed him and, after a kiss like that, he immediately softened up, whereas before that, he'd been sitting there all nervous, his eyes flashing like a tiger's in the night — that's how Grandma Fima expressed it. And Mikheyev stopped arguing with the company, and kissed everyone, although he was slightly embarrassed about it, and then, strange to relate, according to Grandma Fima, Polina, not in the slightest embarrassed, started kissing everyone with great gusto, so that everyone started ooing and ahing and making all sorts of bold suppositions about their future life together, such as whether Mikheyev might not die of exhaustion, to which one-eyed Fomin said that he ought to eat honey and drink fresh milk. But the other Fomin said that that mightn't help, because his nephew had tried to cure himself of exhaustion by running out into the field where the cows grazed and sucking milk straight out of the udder, and the cows liked it, only his nephew still died; it happened a long time ago. Then granddad Yegor said that he remembered another occasion when he toppled into the river out of a boat and he's never been able to swim, and couldn't then either, and it was deep there, and, above his head, while he was turning over and over under the water, he saw the water weaving itself into a sort of hempen sheet, all green mixed up with light, and there was noise all around him under the water, probably the air escaping from him, and then he was suddenly seized by such fear that he started turning over and over like a hobgoblin and somehow or other grabbed hold of the boat and was carried to a shallow spot. Then Postanogov asked him what he meant by his story, and Granddad Yegor thought for a bit and then said he meant that no one knows what's waiting for him where, and perhaps Mikheyev, in his life to come, would also turn head over heels like that — and not be lost. Then everyone burst out laughing, partly at Granddad Yegor and partly at Mikheyev. And that was the last thing the women said about the wedding, near me. Then they plunged me headfirst back into myself, taking away my outlook, and when I came to the surface I heard this word: war.

8. On Sunday — to War

"Hurry up," said Mikheyev to his bustling aunts. "Do hurry up. I know you do things quickly and no one could be any quicker, but today we really have to hurry."

"What are you in such a hurry for?" asked Polina's mother. "The call-up notice hasn't even come yet. They'll call you up when it's time. Why are you in such a hurry to leave your wife, after your very first night?"

Mikheyev was standing in the middle of the room and Polina was embracing him and his eyes were looking all around him, only not at her hair, just under his chin, but at his scurrying aunts and Polina's mother, standing stockstill, like a tree-stump.

"I've got to hurry," he said. "What's a call-up notice? It's just a piece of paper, after all. It could even get lost, or they might forget to write it out. The people sitting over at the enlistment office are inexperienced, things are in rather a mess, bits of paper everywhere. We're a long way from the district center, I could easily get lost in that mess, so of course I have to hurry."

"I was right, not wanting to marry you," whispered Polina. "I was right not wanting to love you. We didn't even have time to be together for a while in our own house, instead of in the forest or down by the river, and you're already hurrying off, you've already begun to live the way you want to, right from the start..."

"Polina," said Mikheyev. "Please try to understand,

Polina. Something in my blood is telling me to do this, and in a hurry."

"How can I undertand you?" whispered Polina. "You've been reading the newspapers and listening to all sorts of nonsense, and now you're the first to go off, and who's asking you to go? Maybe no one except me needs you."

"I give you my word," said Mikheyev. "I didn't pay much attention to the newspapers, I just read bits here and there, now and again, and I know no one except you specially needs me, but something in my blood, my very own blood, is telling me to go now."

"How can I understand you if you keep talking to me in such a vague way?" whispered Polina. "Nothing's telling young Fomin to go, or Postanogov, but something's telling you to."

"You've got your arms around me, so you can't see," said Mikheyev, "but I can see young Fomin's father through the window, pouring water on his head, out of a bucket, to sober him up and inside the house his mother's packing his bag for him, and crying. The fact that nothing's telling Postanogov to go doesn't concern me — it just means he's a different sort of man from me, or the Fomins, but that's what he is and I don't care about him at the moment. I'm in a hurry to go."

"He doesn't love you, Polina," said her mother. "I love you and I'd never do anything like this to you."

"Shut up, mother!" Polina shouted, tearing herself away from Mikheyev. "So he doesn't love me, doesn't he? Be quiet, or I'll leave you, I'll go right away by myself!"

"You'll live with us," replied Mikheyev's two aunts, as they bustled past. "You belong to us now, whether you like it or not."

"I'm not saying anything," said Polina's mother. "I've been watching it all for three months and I haven't said a thing. He's done you wrong and he's still doing you wrong."

"I can't spend any longer here with you," said Mikheyev. "Give me my bag, aunts."

Polina was about to shout something else at her mother, but she looked around at Mikheyev. The look on his face was so purposeful and his features so set, except for his mouth which was clenched so tightly, that his cheekbones stood out more sharply and his eyebrows came slightly together. It was as if he could see something in front of him which he couldn't take his eyes off, something moving about quickly and for no obvious reason, and he had to watch these movements carefully and try to make some sense of them before he could move himself. And they were stopping him, and not giving him his bag right away, talking about something else and trying to divert his attention.

Polina didn't say anything to him, but ran over to the aunts and they quickly got everything he needed together, and then they were already walking through the village together, on their way to the district center, to the enlistment office. Mikheyev was talking and while he talked, his face didn't change.

"I know you'll miss me, but you won't have time to miss me too much, especially when the child is born. You'll find yourself so snowed under with things to do, that I'm actually worried about whether you can cope without me, although you're a sensible girl and know how to put up with things, but you still can't do all the different things a man has to do, so I'll try to get my job done as soon as possible, only it's something I don't know anything about and I should think it would be quite a while before I get used to it and understand it all, a year at least, or perhaps even two, that's why I'm in such a hurry now, so I can get started with it as soon as possible and finish it as soon as possible and come back to you. And then no one will be able to trouble us and we'll live the way we wanted to, even better, because we're both going to miss each other so much, so unbearably, I'm even starting to miss you already, and I want to tell you about how I love you again, how strong my love for you is, and how lucky I am that you're now my wife and can't escape my love, can never escape it now, that's how lucky I am."

"I don't want to get away from you, anywhere," I said, "because I love you, damn you, it's you who's strange and going away from me and saying stupid things to me. I know about everything and understand everything better than you do, and I'll never let you have your own way completely, even when you come back, I don't care what sort of hero you become there, I still won't let you."

"I don't want to become a hero there," said Mikheyev, "because I don't really understand what you have to do to be a hero, my mind's on something quite different, how to get started there as quickly as possible, so I can finish as quickly as possible and get back to you."

"I know about everything and understand everything better than you do," I said. "You're just strange, it was just my particular fate to fall in love with someone strange, who's always kicking against the pricks and getting out of hand and can't even wait one day for the enlistment notice but goes off of his own accord, on a Sunday, when people are supposed to rest and not go off to war. And tonight there'll be guests coming, once they've slept it all off, so they can start having a good time again, and I have to announce to all these good folk that my husband, after the first night, has run off to war."

This is the way she and I talked for the last time, and I went·off to war to fight and wait, and I went home to live and wait, and I watched her go, and I watched him go, and, God in Heaven, how unbearable it was to part. Well, you just wanted to cry out, you wanted to bite your lips, but all we found time to do was to have a little argument, by way of farewell. He was twenty and she was nineteen, and she went off, and he went off — on a Sunday, on a Sunday to war, on a Sunday, do you understand?

9. A General Picture of the War with Some Salient Details

War astounds people, and they close their eyes, not wanting to look at themselves in this mirror of their own imperfections, while bolder people write violent stories, novels, tales and epic poems about war, in order to provide mankind with some facts for contemplation. And mankind contemplates and contemplates — for three thousand years now it has been contemplating the novels and stories, but still not to the point of not firing its guns. This is not a story or a poem about an absolutely happy village, it is simply a song which the author is singing, like one of the old ox-cart drivers in the South, carting wheat to the Crimea, and in the other direction salt. He is singing in the wide expanse of time and space, singing because that's the way he's made, only it's not wheat he's carting, but his own personal load of daily life, but he does travel along singing all the same, what else can I say?

War erupted unexpectedly and started shooting at the whole world, at every living thing, at all the works of man and even at indifferent nature. For Russians, the general picture of the war was at first a completely abominable one because the green-colored Germans with *Gott mit uns* on the buckles of their belts were right outside Moscow, on the

Don, on the Volga, on the Oka, on the Neva, in big cities and in small villages, so that was the abominable picture at first. And it stayed that way for a long time, the summer sun shone, the fall rains came, the snow fell, the earth turned green again and winter whitened, and there was no change.

Then there were changes for the better and there were no more changes for the worse, and that, in a manner of speaking, is the general picture.

As for salient details, there were more than enough. There were as many details as there were people, even more, a lot more.

10. Mikheyev Lies in the Open Field, Growing Accustomed to Things

So this is what this fire-resistant work is all about — there's so much to get to know about it and about weapons, your own and other people's, and about the locality, and there's a lot to get to know about your own body, too, and no one can say in short that you mustn't hurry in doing all this, because sometimes that's precisely what you must do, and at breakneck speed, and sometimes you have to mark time. All around you there is rumbling and noise and hustle and bustle and clouds of dust, all trying to get you muddled up, to confuse you, to make you lose your clarity of thought or else just the opposite, to blind you with excessive clarity, and make you think that suddenly everything is quite simple and you yourself are invulnerable, bullets are afraid of you and bayonets, see, won't go into you.

The Germans fired rarely, lazily and senselessly, so that

in his individual trench Mikheyev enjoyed, in a manner of speaking, perfect peace. He was able to let his thoughts wander from the Germans in front of him, from his preparedness for the unexpected, and from the open field around him, although not completely, of course — his thoughts never wandered completely away, he was too experienced for that, but all the same, enough to allow him to go carefully over the ground he had covered, to recall all the things he knew and check them once again, even his muscles, how which muscle should function in which situation and whether he was quite ready for it to function like that, and whether it might forget to work as it should if something unexpected happened, although Mikheyev himself might lose his presence of mind if something unexpected happened and forget to use the muscle.

This, then, is how he accustomed himself to things, out in the open field, and not for the first time, either, and everyone in the war accustomed himself, gradually, like that in the same way, and the whole country gradually accustomed itself to the unusual situation it found itself in as well, including the village Mikheyev had left behind. And it turned out, gradually, of course, that the devil is not as black as he's painted, and that this is work we can do like any other and, indeed, in the final analysis, probably no worse, and in fact a whole lot better than any other, and there you were imagining to yourselves that we'd never manage. In the final analysis, of course, it's not something that happens straight away — we can't do it straight away, the size of the State is such that we can't do anything straight away, we aren't at all fond of precise deadlines, timetables, regulations and people snapping their fingers and expecting everything just to fall into place.

There's no point in expecting anything like that from us, our country is far too vast for that, it's not something we take to. However, in the final analysis we can do it, one way or another, we don't understand ourselves exactly how...

11. Private Kuropatkin Talks to Mikheyev about Certain Needs He Has

Just before the terrible attack, as a result of which Mikheyev ceased to live here among us, not immediately before the attack, but a week or so before it, when their unit was stationed in a small Ukrainian village, quartered in the few houses the Germans had not set fire to while retreating, or to put it more exactly, in the few houses which had not burnt down, although they'd been set fire to, in the few houses which had, fortunately, been left standing, purely by accident, because the Germans had been in a hurry when they were getting out and hadn't gone about their business as thoroughly as they had when they'd been advancing, well, in one of these houses, where they were lying side by side for the night, Kuropatkin and Mikheyev had a talk.

"What do you keep tossing and turning for, and not sleeping?" Mikheyev asked Kuropatkin softly, and his calm voice, amidst the hard-earned snoring of the other soldiers sounded like singing amidst the beating of drums.

"I'm thinking about certain needs I have, and I can't sleep," said Kuropatkin. "You had time to get married, but I didn't, so you know a lot about women that I don't know. I don't know very much and then only bits and pieces, because up in Yaroslavl, I had relationships with different girls, with three all told, but nothing that lasted, so I don't remember much about it and didn't manage to sort out exactly how it all works. I was in too much of a hurry, but if I had a wife..."

"I feel sorry for you," said Mikheyev. "You're really mixed up, you might say hopelessly mixed up, if that's the way you're looking at it. I can see why you can't sleep. You're so mixed up, no wonder you can't sleep."

"You're right," said Kuropatkin. "I can't. If I lie on my back, it's no good. If I lie on my side, it's worse. If I lie on my stomach it's totally unbearable. And if I turn over on my back it's no good all over again."

"You're really mixed up," said Mikheyev. "You don't understand the difference."

"What difference?" Kuropatkin asked, turning over on his side.

"In peacetime it might be hard to understand the difference, but in wartime only an idiot can't see it. You're a good soldier, a brave lad, you're not slack when it comes to carrying your machine-gun about, but you seem to lack brains, you don't seem to be able to use your brains to understand simple things," said Mikheyev.

"I can't remember anything at all about the first girl, however hard I try. The only memory I've got is of softness and warmth. We found a way into the church — we've got these abandoned churches, this one was called St. Nicholas'-on-the-Marsh, I later found out it was called that even before Lenin — and we lay down on a padded jacket. I can't remember anything about it at all, which is odd, but I can remember the church. It was used for storing things, and before that, it was a canteen, and before that, officers used to get married in it — that was a long time ago, the watchman told me about it when he surprised us. It's odd the rubbish I've remembered, from when the watchman and I were having a smoke, — he said to come there by all means, but she got all embarrassed and then later I lost track of her, so I can't remember a thing. I remember a little more about the second one. We met five or six times.

She was thin, no chest and no behind and slender arms. I remember how she kissed, and I especially remember how she put her long arm around my neck, such a gentle arm it was, her shoulder didn't have any muscles in it — it was as gentle as could be, it began right from the shoulder and had thin veins in it. How about a smoke, Mikheyev, what do you say?"

Kuropatkin turned over on his stomach and lit up.

" You keep talking," said Mikheyev, "and then I'll give you the benefit of a bit of good sense and reason. Don't worry, we'll smarten you up, you're only stupid from being so young, and since that's the case, it'll pass. It's the ones who are old or naturally stupid it's pointless trying to communicate with — they're stupid for life, not like you."

"I can't remember whether she had a braid or not," said Kuropatkin, turning over onto his back. "It's the third one I remember best of all. She was called Olya, although we only slept together four times—it was in the winter and it was cold and there was nowhere to go, so we used to go to a friend of hers, only she had to find somewhere else to go, and this friend had a fierce grandmother, who was a believer and almost never left the house, but once she went to the hospital for a week. This one was a bit fatter, with a figure a bit like our lieutenant-colonel's, except for her chest, which was much bigger, and a tiny bottom, but her sides were wide and so were her shoulders. I can remember her fingers, short fingers, she kept stroking my nose for some reason — she used to touch it with her finger, it was very nice. Only these girls, they were all easy game, took it all a bit lightly, so to speak. So, if I had a wife, I'd know all the niceties, I'd have found out all there was to know, and I could fight this war with more peace of mind and not toss and turn all night. I could lie quietly and remember."

"You're really hopelessly mixed up, if that's how you

think and you put your wife on the same level with other women, " said Mikheyev. "It's just as well you didn't get married — it would've been a disaster, if you can't tell the difference between a wife and someone who isn't your wife."

"They're both women — what difference is there?" Kuropatkin objected. "I can't bring a whole woman to mind. I can imagine one in parts, the stomach, for example, or the legs, or the shoulder-blades, — for me they're all just a lot of white patches, so to speak, and I'm not even talking about the main bit."

"There's an enormous difference," said Mikheyev. "It's like the difference between you and a fascist, although both you and he are men, and on the outside you're exactly the same, and inside you've got the same anatomy, the same kidneys, and even the brain in your heads is made the same, yet the difference between you is a fundamental one — your spirits are different, it's not in the way you're made, physically. There's a difference in spirit between a wife and other women — it's not a matter of external characteristics in the form of breasts, legs or stomach, although even here there might be individual and significant disparities. A woman who isn't your wife exists only for what's outside you, while a wife exists not only for what's outside but also for the spirit, so you can talk and argue with her because, as opposed to a fascist or someone who isn't your wife, there's nothing deceptive about her, — she's yours entirely, whereas her opposite isn't yours entirely, but only on the outside, can you understand the enormous difference?"

"Not very well," said Kuropatkin.

"There you are, you see," said Mikheyev. "You were think-ing of getting married. Until a man understands this dif-ference and grasps it firmly, he shouldn't get married. It would just turn out stupidly — he wouldn't end up with a

solid family for the rest of his life, and it would particularly
be a disaster if an idiot like that had children. It wouldn't
matter what he did, you'd have one great big mess. His wife
would think he looked on her as his wife, and his children
would think he looked on their mother as his wife, and all
their relatives and neighbors and friends would think the
same thing, but he would not be looking on her as his wife,
he'd be searching for another woman to look on as his wife,
but he'd find it hard and even harder to find one, because
he'd already have a wife, and he'd even have children from
his wife, but he wouldn't want a wife, but someone to sleep
with to cool his blood, but sleeping with someone to cool
his blood wouldn't be enough for him, you see, because
without realizing it, he'd be looking for a wife, although he
already had a wife, and the woman he might sleep with
could quite easily turn out to be a wife, too, but some other
husband's wife, and she might be looking for a husband for
herself, for the same reasons as him, but not her own, but
another one, and there you'd have a real disaster in the
making, and his wife wouldn't like it at all, and her husband
wouldn't like it, and their children wouldn't like it, nor
would any of the relatives, neighbors or friends, either,
because they'd already have enough to worry about of their
own — they wouldn't want to have anything to do with that
muddle, a muddle like that would only make life all the
harder for them, and they'd have to try and sort it all out,
they couldn't help trying to sort it all out, they wouldn't be
accustomed to not trying to sort it all out, but it's impossible to sort things out if the two husbands and the two
wives and all their children can't sort out themselves who's
who and who's the real husband and wife and who isn't and
why. Can you understand now what the difference is? Why
aren't you saying anything?"

Kuropatkin made no reply and said nothing, because

he'd gone to sleep.

"You're asleep," said Mikheyev. "That means you've understood it all and calmed down. I told him he wasn't a fool, Polina, just young. See, I turned out to be right."

"Of course you were right," said Polina, "and I'm thinking about that now, too, and it seems strange to me that I was constantly arguing with you before and never agreed with you about anything. But today I agree with you about everything, and you shouldn't be thinking about anything now, except for one thing — how to finish fighting as soon as possible and come back to me, because I haven't got the strength to keep waiting for you, and anyway, our twins have never seen you, and they're both already talking and growing up big and strong, although they don't get enough to eat and they don't eat often. I haven't got the strength to keep waiting for you, either as a wife, or simply as a woman, or as a mother, or with all the work I've got to do. I am left here alone with your sons — my mother's gone, and your aunts have died and I sold the cow for meat — I didn't have the time to look after her, and I'm feeling the strain of all the work, and I can't cope with all I've got to do at home, and the kids are by themselves all day, and the fence is falling apart, and the roof has sprung a leak, and the garden is covered in weeds, please come quickly."

"I'll be back soon, very soon now," said Mikheyev. "We've stopped retreating now and we're going forward instead. We're going quickly, as fast as we possibly can, although the wastage in terms of extra men lost has been enormous, still we have to move quickly, and I'm moving the quickest of all, so that I have the impression I'm advancing at the head of the whole army and everyone is moving along behind me as one man. Be patient for a little while longer, I beg you."

"I'll be patient as long as you like, just so long as you come back alive," said Polina.

"Listen, Mikheyev," said Kuropatkin, waking up. "I should've married that Olya all the same. Now I've gone and dreamt about different exciting white patches again, each one whiter than the next."

But Mikheyev appeared to be asleep and didn't answer him, while around them tired soldiers slept on the floor, having taken off their boots and covered themselves with their great-coats. They were fast asleep, breathing wheezily and with difficulty the heavy air of the room they had filled to overflowing, and these were serious soldiers, with serious weapons fiercely disposed to the enemy even in sleep. This was a real army the people had formed itself into for its own salvation, and not a lot of yellow-beaked new recruits, lost and practically without arms, like the ones who were positioned just over two years before, not far from this village, on the other side of the river, wearing anything on their feet, from sandals to scuffs, with just a few in boots bound with leg-wrappings, having only their immediate commanders with them because the higher-up commanders had lost track of them a long time before, and the division commander himself had lost track of them and had come, with his staff, to the place where his division should have been and it wasn't there and the staff battalion went into battle with the Germans, taking the place of a whole division and failed, of course, to defend anything, including this village, and the Germans overran it, and lots of the inhabitants fled from it and some of them turned up in Mikheyev's village. Parts of their story will be told; however, the story will not be told of how the people got genuinely angry and started fighting in earnest, and how the division commander started fighting in such earnest that he's now a marshal, and perhaps Mikheyev would have told it, if it hadn't been for the attack after which Mikheyev passed from among us.

12. The Attack during which Mikheyev Passed from Among Us

"A long, long time ago everyone, even the ancients, knew that war is work, just as much as growing grain or raising cattle or fitting out a house, except that it's bloody work and that's what makes it unusual. Retreating is work, and so is advancing, and right now we're advancing, doing it, as we've done any other work for a long time now, in a slap-dash fashion, as best we can, in great haste, but this time it was unavoidable and this is why many people have died, so many that no one has yet counted how many, or if someone has counted, he was frightened by the total he got and has kept it to himself. Tomorrow he'll tell us, tomorrow when everything is back to normal and clear, both in real terms and according to the figures, when all shortcomings have disappeared by some mysterious miracle, the fields are cov-ered in ears of corn, fat herds go to the meadows to graze, badly built houses have suddenly turned into crystal pal-aces and faces have broken into happy smiles. Then, in this marvellous tomorrow which we can but put our trust in, and hope for, inasmuch as there's most decidedly nothing else to put our trust in or hope for, in this tardy tomorrow, when the dead rise up again, sins are remitted and hang-men kiss their victims — they'd like to kiss them now, because, from time immemorial in Russia, hangmen have sought the love of their victims, because although they're hangmen, now they'll certainly soon be victims themselves, so hangmen would like to be at one with their victims, movingly united at the fulfillment of a universal-historical act, and they'd like it so much that they don't allow them-selves to contemplate any other possibility — so when the dead rise up again, and sins are remitted, hangmen embrace their victims and fools are simply forgiven, then they'll sort everything out and it will become clear that everything was absolutely right, inasmuch as it was crowned by such stupendous results, attained by means of the conquering of shining heights with the aid of a variety of methods, including work of a slipshod kind. That's why there's no need, at present, to bustle around and attempt to dash forward and take away from future generations absolutely all the work of making sense of our astounding times — we need to leave them, these generations, something to busy themselves with and anyway, why should we carry out yet another piece of work in a slipshod fashion. It would be better for everyone to make some effort himself, according to his capacities, expecting nothing personally for himself for his diligence, not even the Kingdom of Heaven, just a happy tomorrow, that radiant tomorrow when we shall certainly be no more, but all the same that is when life in all its beauty will begin..."

"I don't agree," said Mikheyev, huddling up more closely to the tank they were being borne swiftly along on towards the ford, and the tank was trembling and shaking, as if it were trying to throw them off.

"There's a war on, I know, and war is certainly hard work, I've never had to do anything as hard before, and never will have to. Retreating was hard and advancing is hard, too, but my life is going to be beautiful in our village, and of course it will be even more beautiful because I've got Polina there and I've got two fine, sturdy boys, even if they are twins, and we'll be having other children, and there's land there which is fruitful and abundant, if people don't keep trampling it down, and I've got lots of different things to do there, which I've got two fairly strong arms for, and I've got a head firmly on my shoulders as well, and when I remember our blue, blue river and our blue, blue sky, and our green,

green forest in which my sons will soon be gathering mush-
rooms, squatting looking at some pine-mushroom, for
example, in the shadows, under the grass and leaves, well, I
don't understand anything about tomorrow, why it will be
more beautiful than my life is now or what will be better
about it then than life in my village now — strike me dead,
if I can understand it, although, of course, I do understand
that going along on a shaking tank in full marching order,
to face the fire isn't terribly pleasant and the river up ahead
is a murky river, and the forest up ahead is black and burnt,
and the sky above me is dusty and smoky — it's an ugly sky,
not sky-colored at all. I can understand all that, the obvious
difference, so to speak, but even here, on the tank, I'm not
complaining, I'm just in a hurry. We're all in a hurry, there's
nothing out of the ordinary about that, you always feel like
getting unpleasant work finished as soon as possible."

"What's that thing you've got?" asked Kuropatkin, pointing at the loud-hailer.

"I'm going to give the Germans a bit of propaganda,"
said the man with the loud-hailer.

"What do you mean?" asked Kuropatkin.

"I'm going to say different words to them in German and
then sing a song."

"In German?" asked Kuropatkin.

"Of course."

"Sing it in Russian," Kuropatkin requested.

"It hasn't got Russian words," said the man with the loud-
hailer, "but I'll put it into Russian for you... It goes something like this:

> Germans, we'll feed you
> If you come to us,
> Germans, we'll keep you,
> If you come across.

La-da-di-da
No need for fear,
We're all friends here,
Be of good cheer,
We've lots of Lili Marlenes,
Lots of Lili Marlenes.
Everywhere you look here,
Everywhere you go,
Tum-ta, tum-ta, tum tum,
They'll always say hullo,
They're standing around,
Looking at you,
Waiting for you,
Hoping for you,
All our Lili Marlenes,
We've lots of Lili Marlenes.

"What's that song for?" asked Kuropatkin.

"To make the Germans want to give themselves up..."

"They won't get any Lili Marlenes here, they'll get none of that," said Mikheyev.

"You get different types among the Germans," said the man with the loud-hailer. "All sorts of different types..."

Once the tanks and the infantry on the tanks had forded the murky river, fighting began of a kind Mikheyev, who was long used to being under fire, had never come across before.

Together with the others he was set down on a sandy spit, about thirty meters wide and in front of them there was a high, sheer bank, and up on top of it the German defenses began, and the earth shifted and shuddered from the explosion of our shells falling on their defense line, and it rained down onto the bodies of our men who were establishing a beach-head by digging deep trenches. The tanks moved off to the left, to go up onto the cliff, while the platoon Mikheyev was in was ordered by its commander to dig even deeper into the earth. The beach-head was part of the far-seeing designs of the distant Command, and the soldiers dug in, glad that it was so easy to dig the earth, except that there was almost nothing to reinforce the sides with.

Mikheyev threw out another spade-full of earth and glanced out of the trench. And it was as if by glancing out, he gave a signal.

The earth shuddered, the sky dissolved in gun-powder, the river burst and poured out on all sides. In the distance the tanks suddenly halted, as if rooted to the ground, and disappeared from view, because night had fallen, and the night fought the day, and here and there the day broke through the darkness, in a desperate attempt to hold out for longer than a mere moment, but the murky darkness crushed it out, covering it with earth and overlaying it with smoke, and nothing could be heard except the monotonous roar of explosions. And in the flashes of daylight, a clump of turf flew by, with a piece of charred asp-wood, an arm holding a gun flashed by — the turret of a tank rolled past, a black piece of shell whistled past, looking enormous to Mikheyev. The German artillery had the beach-head covered and began mixing a paste out of the sand, the dead and the living in order to confound the plans of our distant Command.

"This is my moment!" shouted the man with the loud-hailer, in Mikheyev's ear. "I'm going to go and shout at them in German!"

"How can you go anywhere with all this firing going on?" Mikheyev shouted in his ear.

"I have to get closer, otherwise they won't be able to hear me!"

The man with the loud-hailer looked at Mikheyev, gave him a squeeze with the hand that wasn't holding the loud-hailer, climbed out of the trench and disappeared.

Mikheyev huddled up against the heaving wall of the trench, concerned, quite reasonably, about staying alive and knowing that gun-fire like that couldn't go on for long. But he was mistaken. The firing went on and on, there was no end to it, and the day tired of fighting the night and gave up, and the invisible sun hid behind the invisible horizon, and it was only then that the firing ceased and silence began to rumble unbearably. Mikheyev straightened up and looked out. The paste had been mixed thoroughly, not a living soul could be seen anywhere, the dug-outs and trenches had been destroyed almost everywhere, the sand was pink, but not from the sunset, the steep cliff had become even steeper and against the sky Mikheyev caught sight of a head — it was looking around the beach-head, as he was, and sticking up beside the head was the dark shaft of a gun-barrel. Mikheyev took aim, unhurriedly, and fired. The head jerked, then dropped, two arms appeared, the gun fell, the arms clutched the head, as if trying to tear it off, a truck crawled out onto the edge of the cliff to help the head, struggling as it made its last efforts, then the German died, quieted down and slowly rolled down the cliff. And then the earth shuddered again, and Mikheyev once more huddled up against the wall of the trench, surprised that this piece of it with him inside it should be invulnerable to shells and splinters, probably because of some insignificant detail in the surface of the locality. This time the firing didn't go on very long, and when it stopped, night had already fallen, and Mikheyev heard slight splashing sounds on the river and realized that reinforcements were coming.

At dawn, the Germans began mashing the beach-head again and made no less a thorough job of it, and towards evening five or six Germans rushed determinedly down from the top of the cliff and Mikheyev started firing unhurriedly, and someone else was firing at them with a machine-gun from somewhere, probably Kuropatkin, and the last German ran back and leapt up onto the edge of the cliff, gesticulating convulsively, and when he appeared against the sky, Mikheyev fired. The German kept sticking up on the edge for a whole minute, waving his arms around, trying to fall towards his own side, but he couldn't — he arched and fell headlong over the cliff. During the night, new reinforcements arrived by river and once again they were all felled, every last one of them, by the German fire, and it went on like that day after day, it was impossible to say for how long, so that Mikheyev even learned to fall asleep under fire and wake up with the silence, while at night he had to eat and drag the badly wounded to the boats.

By now he had little idea what he was doing, or why he still hadn't been killed. It was inexplicable, and he came to love his secure, seemingly magical corner of the trench, which had become his home. And once when particularly large reinforcements arrived and Mikheyev found out that he was now the commander of the section, he got upset because all ten soldiers of his section couldn't fit into his home in the sand, only four could, and he didn't know who to choose — they were all young, there was almost nothing between them and all of them should have stayed alive. He sat and thought about where to put them all. If they deepened the trench, six men could fit in, perhaps even seven, but three still wouldn't fit in — after all, the whole place was no bigger than a footstool — yet beyond this footstool no one had ever managed to stay alive. But it couldn't be dug any deeper, he'd already dug down to water, you couldn't go down any further, it would all collapse. But he was now the commander, so if he were going to follow the rules honestly, he ought to work to save himself, but he was also obliged to think about those under him, preserve their lives, and make sure they were not lost uselessly, but remained in service. Nor could he give up his own place, it was utterly impossible, it would be stupid from the point of view of his military work. After all, only one soldier could fit into his place — now if four could, it would be a differ-ent matter, because then it would have some sense, but when only one could, it made no sense, but if four could have, he'd have thought about it. In peace time, obviously the man at the top had to accept the worst in every regard, and in a similar situation, he would, of course, give up his own interests and take the heaviest burden on himself, but he didn't know what to do in wartime.

"You see," he said to the soldier, dozing alongside him, "I don't know how to squeeze you all in close to me."

"What?" said the dozing man, waking up with a start. And out of his wide-open, night-time eyes flew fear, pain and hope, and they flew into Mikheyev's eyes.

"I say I don't know what to do," said Mikheyev, frowning from being scratched by someone else's fear, pain and hope. "I don't know how to squeeze you all in here, because here you've got more chance of staying alive, but we don't all fit and I don't know what to do."

But the soldier had already dozed off again and wasn't listening to words which, at that moment, he had absolutely no need of.

13. Mikheyev Talks to the Earth

"I thought over a lot of things while your surface was keeping me alive," said Mikheyev. "This is one of them. If I knew
that this great big shell was going to explode somewhere,
no matter where, and I knew that my trench was safe and
would withstand even an explosion like that which nothing
could withstand anywhere, and everything in the world
would be destroyed and everyone living in the world would
die, and I could only fit four people into my trench, then
of course first of all I'd take in Polina and my two sons, but
I'd crawl out just the same and go off somehow just the
same, to make room for other children who hadn't yet lived
nearly as long as I had, and, anyway, I'd feel uncomfortable
about surviving, although things would be more than difficult for Polina without me, especially since this shell
would destroy everything, the proletarians of all lands, and
the capitalists, and an enormous amount of work would be
left undone."

"A tremendous amount," said the earth.

"Exactly," said Mikheyev. "All the same, I'd have to leave
the trench, although then Polina would have to build her
own house and dig her own garden, and milk the cow, and
make clothes for the kids and teach them to read and write.
But, you see, the shells that are going to start falling on us
in the morning are different from that enormous shell only
in the force of the explosion, not in essence."

"Of course, not in essence," said the earth.

"And, since that's the case," said Mikheyev, "it means that
my decision shouldn't be any different in essence, either.
After all, these soldiers who I at present, unfortunately,
have direct authority over, also want to stay alive and they
have a right to stay alive, but tomorrow they'll start killing

them off, almost uselessly. In the case I mentioned before, I wouldn't just crawl out of the trench but I'd run to where they were getting ready to fire the shell and try to stop them firing it. There's no point dying senselessly like a fly, and leaving Polina to work. It means, in the end, that I should do the same thing now, I should leave here the seven men who will survive and run as fast as possible with the other three to where they're shooting at us from. There's nothing else left for me to do."

"No, there's nothing else left for you to do," said the earth, with difficulty.

14. The Attack during which Mikheyev
Passed from among us

Quickly, in the darkness, across the bloodied sand, and further on, across the crumbly earth at the foot of the cliff, ran four soldiers. They crawled up like grass snakes over the edge and disappeared. However, our sentry noticed them on the bank and shook his superior awake.

"Comrade lieutenant!" he said. "We're attacking! Our men have gone in!"

"Get the platoon commanders!" ordered the officer.

Some time later, firing started up in the German position, flares soared up into the sky, the noise of battle reached our troops on the other bank of the river, and as happens in a war all the time the suddenly roused mechanism came into action, drawing in more and more people, going ahead of, and destroying, plans and designs, bursting into flame, as if of its own accord, without appropriate preparations, when the artillery for an advance had still not been grouped in position, and tanks had not been assembled in the necessary numbers, and the signallers hadn't got the communications working, and all the different kinds of troop commanders hadn't co-ordinated their actions or given assignments to those under them, or shown them the targets, the time limits or the reference points. Yet the cannons were firing and the personnel carriers were moving forward and planes were flying on sorties and sappers were setting up a bridge and the signallers were laying a cable and the commanders were pointing out targets, time limits and reference points.

In the German trenches, the four soldiers were fighting frantically, not trying to capture anything or dig in anywhere, but forcing their way ever forward, creating confusion in the German defenses and alarm in hearts and causing hasty, rushed reactions. But there are no miracles in a war, or almost never any, and it was impossible for four men to break through the defenses, impossible to beat a hundred enemies — all that was possible was for them to die a hero's death.

"Your husband died a hero's death," Polina read and she didn't cry out, didn't fall down, but kept standing like an arrow. She just leaned against the house and stood there, motionless, not wanting either to move, speak, cry or live.

15. Private Kuropatkin Is Brought before the Officers in an Unknown Glade Several Months Later

"Can you tell us, Private," said the old colonel, "why it was that you didn't fight?"

"I did fight, Comrade Colonel," the private replied. "I

directed uninterrupted machine-gun fire at the barn, as indicated — those were my orders."

"But there was no one in the barn, there was no one on the farm at all, in fact there was no one anywhere within ten kilometers of the farm," said the colonel, wearily. "Not a single German, do you understand?"

"I understand, Comrade Colonel."

"If you understand, why were you shooting?"

"Those were my orders, Comrade Colonel."

"I don't know what to do," said the young major to the captain and the *zampolit*.* For four hours, a platoon attacks a barn containing no one and a farm also containing no one — in fact there was no one within ten kilometers of the farm — the attack went on for a whole day, yet it's impossible to find who's to blame."

"Surely you could see that there was no one there?" said the colonel.

"Yes, Comrade Colonel, I could!" said Kuropatkin cheerily. "I'm no fool, of course I could see that!"

"Then why did you fire, if you could see that?" asked the captain.

"Permission to reply, Comrade Colonel?" asked Kuropatkin, turning to the superior officer.

"Carry on."

"The order was given, Comrade Captain."

"And then what happened?" asked the major.

"Permission to reply, Comrade Colonel?"

"Carry on."

"Then, carrying out our orders, we made a dash in a vehicle for the lake, Comrade Major," said Kuropatkin. "The order was given to take the boundary and hold it. I held it, the others didn't manage it, they were killed."

"There was a General Kuropatkin," said the *zampolit*.

---

* *Zampolit:* a senior officer, responsible for political propaganda and education.

"Was he a relative of yours?"

"Permission to reply, Comrade Colonel?"

"Carry on," said the colonel. "You can reply without asking me."

"Actually, I need to ask something, Comrade Colonel. Permission to ask a question, Comrade Colonel?"

"And you can ask questions without asking," said the colonel.

"I don't understand, Comrade Colonel!" said Kuropatkin. "May I ask the question?"

"I've already said you can. Ask it without asking!" The colonel was beginning to get unsettled.

"I don't understand, Comrade Colonel!"

"What don't you understand, private? What?" asked the colonel.

"I don't understand 'ask it without asking,' Comrade Colonel!"

"Ask him," the colonel said, pointing to the *zampolit*, "don't ask me," and here the colonel jabbed the same finger at himself.

"Permission to speak, Comrade Colonel: he's not the one I need to ask," Kuropatkin said, pointing to the *zampolit* with his chin, "you are," and here he pointed at the colonel, with his chin.

"Carry on," said the colonel, shrugging his shoulders.

"Where does Comrade General Kuropatkin come from?" asked Kuropatkin.

"How would I know?" said the colonel. "What has General Kuropatkin got to do with it?"

"Comrade *zampolit* asked if Comrade General Kuropatkin was a relative of mine, Comrade Colonel," said Kuropatkin. "That's why I'm inquiring where he came from, because if he's from my part of the world, it's very likely that he is a relative, but if he's not from my part of the world, then it's not so likely that he's a relative, Comrade Colonel."

"Where are you from, Comrade?" the colonel asked the *zampolit,* severely.

"Yaroslavl," said the *zampolit,* surprised.

"I'm from Yaroslavl, too!" said Kuropatkin, joyfully. "Permission to report, Comrade Colonel, I'm from Yaroslavl, too!"

"So what?" asked the colonel.

"Well, Comrade Colonel, if our comrade here is from Yaroslavl and Comrade General Kuropatkin is also possibly from Yaroslavl, and I'm from Yaroslavl, then it works out that we're all from Yaroslavl, so possibly we're all related," Kuropatkin explained.

"My name is Krasnov, not Kuropatkin," said the *zampolit.* "And, anyway, I was only born in Yaroslavl, I lived in Saratov."

"So what?" the colonel asked him.

"So I can't be related to General Kuropatkin," grinned the *zampolit.*

"I don't understand," said the captain. "Why, if you lived in Saratov, can't you be related to General Kuropatkin?"

"Which of you, then, is related to General Kuropatkin?" asked the colonel.

"I don't know, Comrade Colonel", said Kuropatkin.

"Perhaps the private is related and I'm not," said the *zampolit.*

"What I don't understand is what your living in Saratov has got to do with anything," said the captain.

"And why does Private Kuropatkin call the White General Kuropatkin comrade?" asked the major, pointedly.

"Silence!" shouted the colonel. "Everyone keep quiet. Talk one at a time, I can't understand a thing you're saying! You talk," he said, indicating Kuropatkin.

"What will I say, Comrade Colonel?" asked Kuropatkin.

"What did you want to say?" asked the colonel.

"I wanted to say I don't know, Comrade Colonel."

"What don't you know?" asked the colonel. "Ask if you don't know!"

"What will I ask, Comrade Colonel?"

"Ask what you don't know, Private Kuropatkin!" ordered the colonel.

"I don't know yet what it is I don't know, Comrade Colonel."

"Comrade Major, take it from the beginning again," said the colonel wearily.

"Yes, sir," said the major. "Well, then, what happened is that our comrade here, the *zampolit,* asked the private if he, that is to say, the private, were related to General Kuropatkin..."

"To hell with General Kuropatkin!" shouted the colonel. "Get to the point of this thing!"

"I seem to remember there's another General Kuropatkin on the First Byelorussian Front," said the captain suddenly. "Not the White general the *zampolit* had in mind, but our own Soviet General Kuropatkin."

"How do you know, captain, that I had the White general in mind, and not our own?" asked the *zampolit.*

"You yourself were surprised that the private should've called a White general comrade," said the captain.

"I wasn't the one who was surprised, it was the major who was surprised," said the *zampolit.*

"So it doesn't surprise you that the private should call the White General Kuropatkin comrade?" the major asked the *zampolit.*

"Silence!" shouted the colonel, even more loudly. "I don't want to hear the name Kuropatkin again! Kuropatkin! Kuropatkin! What's Kuropatkin got to do with it?"

"Kuropatkin is his name," said the captain.

"Captain, that's enough!" shouted the colonel. "I forbid anyone to mention Kuropatkin!"

"What you have forbidden us to mention is his name," said the captain.

"Whose name?" asked the colonel.

"This private's name," said the major. "And if you've forbidden us to speak about him, then what are we going to speak about?"

"We'll never get anything sorted out at this rate," said the colonel. "Take it from the beginning, major. And I forbid you to mention that name, is that clear?"

"Yes, sir," said the major.

In the glade, seated at a table, at the entrance to the shelter, the four officers fell to thinking about who was to blame for the platoon being wiped out, while Private Kuropatkin stood before them in a submissive pose and tried to help them.

"Who ordered the platoon to attack the farm and the barn?" asked the colonel.

"I did," said the captain. "On the battalion commander's order."

"There was no mention in the order I gave about your having to attack a farm which was empty and a barn which was even emptier," said the major.

"Exactly," said the captain. "There was no mention of its being empty, but it was said that there were Germans there."

"Where did you get the idea, Comrade Major, that there were Germans in the barn and on the farm?" asked the colonel.

"From the order given to the regiment," shrugged the major.

"The farm wasn't mentioned in the order to the regiment!" said the colonel.

"But the target area was, and the farm is within the target area," objected the major.

"And you didn't know that there was no one there?" asked the colonel.

"No, I didn't," said the major.

"And you didn't know?" the colonel asked the captain.

"No, I didn't," said the captain.

"Nor did you know, naturally," said the colonel, waving an arm at the *zampolit.* "So who knew?"

"I did, Comrade Colonel!" said Kuropatkin.

"How did you know?" asked the colonel.

"The night before the battle, if you'll permit me to report, Comrade Colonel, I went there to relieve myself!" said Kuropatkin.

"Where did you go? What do you mean?" asked the colonel.

"To the barn, Comrade Colonel."

"Why did you go there to relieve yourself?" asked the colonel. "Where there were Germans positioned?"

"Excuse me, Comrade Colonel, there were no Germans there!"

"This looks suspicious," said the *zampolit.* "How did you know that there weren't any Germans there?"

"Don't interrupt me," said the colonel. "So you knew there were no Germans there. Then why did you fire at the barn for four hours?"

"Carrying out the task we'd been given, Comrade Colonel."

"And who was it that gave you this idiotic task?" asked the colonel.

"The platoon commander in person, Comrade Colonel!"

"And did you tell him that there was no one there?"

"I certainly did."

"And what did he say?"

"He told me to bugger off, Comrade Colonel!"

"And what did you say?"

"I said yes, sir, Comrade Colonel."

"And what did he say?"

"He said the same thing again, and also that everyone knew there were Germans there — the regimental commander, the battalion commander and the company commander — and I was just trying to be smarter than everyone else."

"And what did you say?"

"Nothing else, Comrade Colonel."

"You didn't tell him you'd relieved yourself there?"

"He didn't ask about that, Comrade Colonel, he went off."

"Do you understand what you did?" asked the colonel. "You alone knew that there were no Germans there and yet you didn't resist, you didn't defend the correct point of view."

"He was carrying out an order," said the captain in his defense.

"We'll get around to you, captain," said the colonel. "You're not educating your soldiers properly."

"That's the *zampolit's* affair," said the major.

"And yours, major, and yours," said the *zampolit*.

"The *zampolit* saved the situation, taking on himself the command of the assault team," said the colonel. "And this soldier is to blame for the loss of the platoon. Do you see that, Private?"

"Yes, Comrade Colonel," said Kuropatkin. "I should've made it clear to our lieutenant that I'd relieved myself there."

"Exactly," said the colonel. "And if your lieutenant hadn't understood, you should've gone to the captain, the major, even me, and got the truth out in the open. You have to fight for the truth, under any conditions, but you threw in the towel. It was an idiotic order, is that clear?"

"Yes, sir."

"Because of you, the platoon was lost," said the colonel. "That was your doing."

"But he was carrying out an order," said the captain, in his defense, again.

"That's not the point," explained the *zampolit*. "He was obliged to carry out the order. The point is that he didn't fight against the order, while simultaneously carrying it out. I trust, captain, that you understand the dialectic here? You must fight against it, while carrying it out — what could be clearer than that?"

"Indeed," said the major. "That's precisely what we need — everyone fighting together against stupid orders, while simultaneously carrying them out."

"I can't altogether agree with you," said the colonel. "In that case, it would be very difficult to find the one to blame, while this time we've succeeded in doing just that, quite quickly."

"But, in this situation, there wouldn't be anyone to blame, at all," said the major. "Because everyone would be equally to blame, from the private to the general."

"No, said the *zampolit*. "Generals couldn't be to blame, because they'd also be fighting against orders, against their own incorrect orders, while simultaneously demanding that they be carried out. That's where the dialectic comes in. There wouldn't be anyone to blame at all, everyone would be fighting against the orders."

"We've digressed," said the colonel. "Something must be decided, concerning this soldier. Let's start with you, Captain. What do you suggest?"

"I suggest that, when the reinforcements arrive, we put

him in a new platoon, as a machine-gunner," said the captain.

"I suggest sending him to a punitive battalion," said the major.

"I suggest he be shot in front of his platoon," said the *zampolit.*

"I agree," nodded the colonel. "That's what we'll do. Private Kuropatkin!"

"Sir!"

"Since you are to blame for the loss of your platoon, you're to be sent to a punitive battalion!"

"Yes, sir, to a punitive battalion!"

"You're dismissed," said the colonel, and Kuropatkin smartly left the unfamiliar glade.

"In the army, everything is so much simpler," said the *zampolit.* "In peace time, it's going to be difficult to find who is to blame among those not fighting against orders."

"Well, I don't have to give orders in peace time," said the colonel. "So I won't lose any sleep over that."

"All the same, it's interesting," said the captain, looking at the *zampolit.* "I wonder where General Kuropatkin does come from? I must find out."

16. Polina at the End of Her Tether

"Curse those wretched boys — I spent a whole hour looking for them out in the yard, in the garden, in the street, and going round the neighbors. I was worried out of my mind about where they'd disappeared to, and they'd got into the stove and closed the door on themselves, pretending it was a cave, and then they went to sleep in there, in the darkness and the soot, and when they'd had a good sleep, they crawled out of it, all hungry, their eyes bright in faces black with soot, and ate potatoes and cabbage while they made plans to disappear off somewhere else, and they're growing bigger, and not just every day, and not just every hour, and what from, I'd like to know — all they get is cabbage, it's lucky I managed to get some potatoes — yet they keep on growing like Ilya Muromets.* I probably made a mistake calling the elder one Ilya, I can't get enough food to feed them.

"Curse that wretched foreman in the workshop, one-eyed smart aleck that he is, who's put me onto the night shift for a whole week. Now I've got to walk four kilometers through the mud, in the darkness, to the station, — it wasn't enough that I had to stand for an hour in the train, now I have to stand with wet feet. I'm always stumbling into puddles in the darkness — you should try it, Mikheyev, why did you have to die a hero's death, — it would've been better if you'd lived the life of the not so heroic, the same as everyone else. I'm at the end of my tether, can't you see that, and the foreman won't leave me alone. You're *healthy,* he says, you're stronger than the others. If you don't come to the storeroom with me, I'll send you to work in the factory garden. But how can I go without the boys, they can't do anything for themselves, except get lost.

"Curse this wretched train, which is always crammed full. There's nowhere to sit down, and people sleep sitting down and standing up. It doesn't matter whether they're on their way to the factory or home from the factory, whether it's a winter's night or summer's day, in the heat or the cold, in the stuffy air. Curse this wretched train, this wretched train, this wretched train. I don't know what, this wretched train, to do, to do, to do, this wretched train, this wretched train,

---

*Ilya Muromets: a Russian folk hero of Herculean proportions.

this belt, can't breathe, Mikheyev, loosen it, that's better, thank you, let me lean on you, how kind you are, Mikheyev, now you can look after the children and feed them, it's ages since I've eaten properly, too, it'll be easier now, I just mustn't jerk, I mustn't jerk, why did I jerk, you're not here now, you're never here at all, all there is is this train, this train.

"Curse this wretched roof, which leaks and this garden, where I haven't earthed up the potatoes or done the weeding. Curse this wretched washing I have to do, and the stove I have to set, and the cabbage I have to boil, and the shop I have to use my ration card in, and the floor I have to wash, and the factory I have to work in endlessly, and the well I have to bring the water back from, and the shoulder-yoke which presses down on my thin shoulders, my tired back and everything that once was yours, Mikheyev. What am I to do, tell me, go on, don't say nothing, tell me, you used to tell me lots of things, say something."

"There is something I can say, right now," said Mikheyev to her. "I'm perfectly willing to say something, it's fools who leave and say nothing. I'll tell you, I want to say something, particularly since I can now see lots of things more clearly than before. My outlook has broadened, I've become really clever now, so that I can tell you very simply and directly what you must do. Before I couldn't have told you so simply, but now I can, because lots of things I now know and understand I didn't know or understand before — my personality got in the way, but it doesn't get in the way now. You need to bring someone home with you, Polina, that's just what you need to do."

"I can't do that, why are you suggesting stupid things like that again, and why did I get to know only you, and start obeying you!" said Polina, while the train rocked and jolted her, rocked and jolted, but people were standing packed in around her, so she couldn't fall over. "I love you, just as I used to, you know, in fact I love you even more. I look at the boys — and love you. I look into the well with the pole and bucket as I lower the bucket into the water, and love you. I look at the poplar and love you, I look at the river, as I do the washing, and love you, and I can't bring anyone else home, because I love you, yet it's you who are suggesting these stupid things to me. Perhaps it isn't you talking to me, perhaps it's me talking to myself?"

"Don't misunderstand me, Polina," said Mikheyev. "You need to do it so both my sons and you can have a proper life, so the house doesn't fall down, the roof leak, the fence topple over, so the potatoes get earthed up, the washing done, the stove set, the floors washed and new glass gets put in the smashed window, and you haven't even realized all the things that need to be done. Your boots, for instance, are in a terrible state, they should be mended. Why do you walk around with wet feet all the time — you'll get rheumatism — and that sour, cabbage barrel of yours is hardly holding together, the top hoop has snapped, a new one should be fitted. And you haven't got enough wood in — it won't even last to mid-winter, you must go to the forest and get some brushwood, and find another horse and bring back some wood, and the wood must be sawn and chopped. And Ilya and Alyosha can't lend you a hand, so it's impossible for you to do without someone else in the house, quite impossible..."

"I realized all that before you told me, don't imagine I didn't," said Polina. "The foreman promised to get me some boots, when the army disposals arrive, and I'll tie up the barrel for the time being with some string. It'll hold together for a while longer, but I don't know what to do about the wood, there's no time left. Anyway, there's no one for me to bring home with me, after you I can't look at anyone else, there's something wrong with all of them, I don't like any of them, and where am I going to find some-one who hasn't got anything wrong with him, and who'll take me with two sons?"

"You'll find someone," said Mikheyev. "I know you will. As for the fact that you love me, there's nothing wrong with that, it makes me feel good, and you'll love me for the rest of your life and that'll only make things better for you."

"I'm sick and tired of listening to these stupid things you're telling me," said Polina. "I'm at the end of my tether."

17. The Children Go to the Forest by the River

By day in the sky above the village, instead of stars, birds and clouds sparkle sonorously in the sun above the golden stems of corn, making life unbearably beautiful, making it beautiful with the depths of its heights, and the smooth flowing of a sense of things that cannot be born in anyone's head apart from the birds and the sky, the river, the clouds and the village, but is simply all these things taken together — the depths of the heights, and the boundless spaces beneath, and human life, which is intertwined with the spaces beneath and the heights above, so tightly inter-twined with the village, the road, the glances of eyes and the turning of hands to work that no bastard can shatter or debase it.

Children can't grasp this sense of things with their minds — the powers of cogitation they need for it still haven't formed in their heads. All they can do is look at the sky with its birds or at the river with its dark, green strands of ooze near the banks, or at the forest, where stillness walks among the tree trunks, and feel, when they've looked, an urgent need to jump around, to tell fantastic stories, to climb over impossibly high fences and to be alive in every way, alive in an interesting way, waving their arms about. So children don't understand this separate sense of things. They're still not grown up enough to have a separate sense of things. They are part and parcel of this sense themselves, whereas grown-ups learn in part to grasp this sense of things, but those who do grasp it are no longer part of that sense, because, in order to grasp it, you have to look at this sense of things from the side, which means you have to step outside it. And it's difficult for those who grasp it to explain it to children, because it's difficult to make children step outside this sense of things, while those who don't grasp it obviously can't explain this sense of things to children, since they don't even understand it themselves. Yet grown-ups are very bad at being alive in an interesting way, and throwing their arms about — that's why, by day, beneath the sky and its flying birds, grown-ups are of no use to children. They just get in the way, and if a grown-up appears on the horizon, children don't pay him any attention, unless he lights a fire or stands on his head.

There were no grown-ups on the horizon and the children of the village, in their small pack, felt alive and free, as they made their way towards the forest.

The vital forces Slavka Postanogov possessed made him the children's marshal, although, admittedly, Kostya Fomin could run much faster, and Vasya Prokhorov was much bigger, and Valka the refugee told much more interesting stories than their teacher, Fyodor Mikhailovich, because he didn't make them remember what he told them.

"We didn't leave straight away," Valka the refugee told them, "because Mama didn't believe the Germans would come, but then they started shooting, and one of their bombs suddenly went off in the neighbor's yard. I even stepped back from the window, I didn't like it, standing near the window. Then we left, after all, because the horses could've been killed. Mama said we'd move away a bit, to where they weren't shooting. And on the road, there were lots of people leaving, they were riding on all sorts of things, even on bullocks, and we were the last of all, and Mama kept looking back. And all around us, they were firing. We went about a hundred kilometers and then suddenly there was this German plane. It flew right at us and started shooting at us, and everyone started running, the horses took off in all directions, there was dust everywhere, people were yelling and I lost my head and lay down on the bottom of the cart. Mama turned our horses off the road, straight into a field, and they galloped off. The cart was shaking terribly, I even shut my eyes tight. Then it got quiet, and when I looked, I saw we were in a forest. It was frightening, and the road behind us was full of holes and puddles, and in front of us was a cart, which had tipped over and the horses were lying there dead, and there was this little wooden shed thing there, lying on its side, and there was no one around. Just Pashka here, sitting beside the cart, really frightened he was, sitting there all by himself."

"I was not frightened," said Pashka. "I was just sitting there."

"Mama went to have a look around, but there was no one anywhere. She walked about in the forest and called out — no one. Then she put the shed thing in the cart with us and sat Pashka in it and we went back, and then went on further, until we got here to you."

"Did you see any Germans?" asked Slavka Postanogov.

"No," said Valka. "I missed out. All I saw was the plane."

"I saw some Germans," said Pashka, "and partisans, too."

"In your dreams, was it?" asked Slavka.

"In my dreams, too," said Pashka.

"Just fancy, so did I," said Vasya Prokhorov. "Can you throw a stone and hit that quail?"

Hanging tremulously in the sky was a quail, crimson in the light-blue sky under white, gold-edged clouds, and Valka, the refugee, threw a stone into the sky, but the stone didn't come anywhere near the quail, which paid the stone no attention. All the boys started throwing, but no one could reach the quail, or even frighten it, occupied as it was with its own observations and its own personal and deeply meaningful trembling. The boys left it in tremulous peace and came to the forest, where a green box-wood shed was standing in some bushes, the same one Valka and his mother and Pashka, whom they'd picked up on the way, sheltered in for the night, from the bad weather, Pashka who had lost his parents in the German bombing raid and still couldn't find them, and no one made any enquiries after him, either.

In the shed, the boys kept supplies of wooden arms, forest nuts and pine-cones, and here lived a forest tortoise, tied up through a hole in his shell. Here they lit fires and roasted potatoes, if they managed to get any, and here in the quietness of the forest grown-ups didn't hinder their growing up on their own.

But now, within close range of the shed, there stood a man. He stood there, leaning against the trunk of a birch-tree, as if it were a door-post, with his legs, in their tarpaulin boots, crossed, unhurriedly rolling himself a cigarette. He had a gray soldier's greatcoat thrown over his shoulders, the collar of his shirt was undone, and he didn't have a cap covering his dark hair. His face couldn't be seen, his face couldn't be made out, and the children's hearts froze, because any man in a greatcoat reminded them of HIM, the one real man, the most important of all men, who somewhere, in unknown regions, was accomplishing heroic feats and from whom there sometimes came, or could come, triangular-shaped letters, written in indelible pencil.

The boys stopped in front of him, but he kept on rolling his cigarette, and then he lit it, straightened his greatcoat on his shoulders and set off, into the depths of the forest, without taking any notice of the boys, as if he hadn't seen them. He walked further and further away, but he didn't grow any smaller, or more inconspicuous — quite to the contrary. He grew and became bigger in the eyes of the boys staring after him. His gray greatcoat blazed and streamed over his shoulders, like the wind, like a flame, he overshadowed the trees in the forest and walked through them. Then, suddenly, he turned around.

Why was this man raising his hand? To threaten, to call, to beckon? To say farewell? To ask forgiveness and take leave? Do you forgive? So long, farewell. Farewell, so long as you forgive. What can be done about the fact that I, like so many others, take leave of you forever — forgive me forever, even though that's a hard thing to do. I don't enjoy having to go away and that's why I'm doing it in silence — this way you'll remember me better as I am, unclouded by words, lifting my hand in farewell. Say farewell wordlessly, just raise your hand, in forgiveness of those staying behind.

And above the shed, the forest made quiet noises, rain spattered down from the thundercloud, which had quickly loomed above, and the drops of water, slipping from the leaves, tapped on the wood.

"Did you see the stripes he had?" Valka, the refugee, asked Slavka.

"Yes, I did," said Slavka. "Seriously wounded five times."

"Six times, not five," said Kostya Fomin.

"Where's he off to?" asked Vasya Prokhorov. "Do you think he's been demobilized?"

"We should've followed him," said Slavka. "But you were all too frightened to."

Pashka, the refugee, was lying propped on his elbow, thoughtfully tracing a line with his finger on the tortoise's shell, making some kind of incomprehensible pattern on it, no doubt a very sad one, because Pashka's face was sad and his finger was sad, too.

"Do you want to play soldiers?" asked Slavka.

"I don't feel like it," said Valka.

"It'd be more fun to build a bonfire," said Vasya.

"Couldn't be bothered," said Slavka. "Why not collect pine-cones?"

"Couldn't be bothered," said Valka.

"Pity we didn't follow him," said Slavka.

"Couldn't be bothered," said Vasya, and his lips trembled.

18. Private Kuropatkin's Night in Novoyelnya

On the western edge of a small town, beside a fence overgrown with hops, stood Private Kuropatkin. He stood there openly, fiddling with his machine-gun, while on the other side of the fence were some young women, five in number, and they were keeping their eye on him. Then one of the women asked him:

"Why are you in such a hurry to leave us, don't you like it here?"

"It's all right, but I have to keep on the move, I can't hide out anywhere for long..."

"Which way are you headed?" asked one of the women.

"West," said Kuropatkin.

"Fancy that," said one of the women.

"I've adjusted to the life," said Kuropatkin. "For example, I can't swim, although I grew up on the Volga, yet the first decoration I got was for crossing a river."

"You don't say," said one of the women.

"You have to be able to get out of any situation safe and sound," said Kuropatkin. "I got across..."

"How did you do it?" asked one of the women.

"There was this dead horse floating around near the bank, and there weren't any other means of getting across close at hand," said Kuropatkin. "I was the first to reach the edge of the river, the others, who could swim, weren't running as fast, but I was running so fast it was hard to stop and I just kept going and jumped straight onto the horse, pulled out my spade and started paddling. And the horse got me to the other side. It made it..."

"Well, fancy that!" said one of the women.

"That's nothing, now the second decoration I got, that was really something," said Kuropatkin. "No dead horse this time, this was a real test of my whole training. I was transferred to the Guards..."

"Tell us about it, if it's interesting," said one of the women.

"Sounds interesting," said the others.

"We were trying to take this town called Novoyelnya," said Kuropatkin. "We'd been trying for ages, but couldn't take it, no matter what we did, and so I was sent to get someone we could make talk, that is to say, a live German. So late that night, this other guy and I crept into Novoyelnya and lay low. Then we saw these two Germans nip into one of the houses. We waited until it was completely dark and then ducked into the house. It was dark, you couldn't see a thing, and I yelled out — Halt! Hände hoch!, and one German, as naked as the day he was born, was out the window and away, but the other one, who was also naked as the day he was born, we stuck in a blanket, gagged and carried off. We carried him along, quietly and quickly, quite a distance, too, taking turns at carrying him on our backs. Then I tripped on something, and in a whisper, pronounced a few unpronounceable words. Suddenly, our prisoner started jerking and twitching and pushed the gag out of his mouth and said in a low voice: "Hey, boys, who are you?" I chucked him down under a bush and lit a torch to have a good look at him and it wasn't a German, but a woman."

"A woman?" asked one of the women.

"Don't interrupt," said the others.

"A real life-sized woman," said Kuropatkin. "We said, what are we to make of this? And she said, my husband and I are partisans, and we got dressed up as Germans and hid for the night, because at dawn we've got things to do, but what am I going to do now, naked as the day I was born, and you put out that torch. And we said to her, you've mucked up our whole operation, and what's your name? And she said, you carry me back there, it's too cold for me to walk in bare feet. And we said, we wanted a German, and she said, why did you yell out in German, that's what caused all the confusion, my name is Ksana, and carry me back as quickly as you can. I've got washing waiting to be done, my husband will be looking for me and we've got this thing planned."

"Well, did you?" asked one of the women.

"Yes, we did," said Kuropatkin. "So long as we thought she was the German we wanted it wasn't hard to carry her, but on the way back she got heavy and awkward to carry."

"Nothing like that has ever happened to me," said one of the women.

"And it never will," said Kuropatkin. "We've liberated you for good."

"Why was this woman so heavy for you to carry?" asked

one of the women.

"Goodness knows, she seemed to have got bigger," said Kuropatkin. "We carried her, holding on to the two ends of the blanket."

"Did they decorate you for what you did at Novoyelnya?" asked one of the women.

"Yes, that's right," said Kuropatkin. "The same night we got an officer, he was wandering around, not being careful enough. They're not fighting too well now, they're desperate. We were angry, and we made him walk in front of us, and he walked all the way to the front line, and it wasn't till we got there that we carried him a bit."

"You must've gotten tired, that night in Novoyelnya," said one of the women.

"That was nothing," said Kuropatkin. "I would've gotten more decorations and learned to fight more quickly if my oldest friend and unforgettable comrade Mikheyev had been with us..."

"Who's he?" asked one of the women.

"He's not with us, anymore," said Kuropatkin. "He died a hero's death, before I got into this...shock battalion."

"What do you mean, shock battalion?" asked one of the women.

"What are we standing around here for, come back to the house, we can sit a while," said one of the women.

"Have a rest at her place and then let's go over to my place," said one of the women.

"I want to give you a tobacco pouch, I made it myself," said one of the women.

"I didn't know how to stand up for the correct point of view then," said Kuropatkin, as he jumped over the fence. "But Mikheyev was no longer with us by that time. So, carrying out my orders, I directed uninterrupted machine-gun fire..."

19. A General Picture of the War with Receding Details

The war was far from over, but it was moving away to the west, and it kept moving further and further away, which was the best direction to move in, leaving its memory behind in our land, and pride in our feelings as a people for a long time, for centuries. And it is impossible not to share this pride it left behind in our feelings as a people, once it's understood that it is not barren thoughts which lead a man to the truth, but communion with the life of people close to him, and not those far away, people of his native soil, and not of foreign soil — it's here that he will find communion, and common concern and his lot in life, and a plot of earth will be his here, forever, at the allotted time, forever.

The war also left misery behind it, the sister of pride. They have one foundation and one root — as it softens, this root gives birth to misery, and as it hardens, it gives birth to pride, and it is better not to go too deeply into all this, because you'll only get entangled in the shoots this root sends out.

The people saved themselves, so why shouldn't they respect themselves for this? An individual man, educated and mortal, may, of course, be above all of life's vanities, above the passions of the people, — what do they matter to him, his life is short, — but the people will live forever and the people will remember all those who smote death with their own death, who gained immortality in the life of the people.

Just beyond a forest farm, beside the road, is a mound, grown over with grass — a soldier's grave. Some women, caring for it in their particular way, put a cross of two birch branches, bound with lime bast, on the mound. Time will go by, and many people, having grown hard, will remember the dead by visiting only the famous cemeteries, where thousands and thousands have been buried in one place. Only thousands and thousands will awaken their feelings. But we, in our song, as we take leave of war forever, because it is passing out of our song, freeing the path of love and life, from all the details of the war, will remember this grave, just around a corner in the forest.

20. Franz, Where Are You?

What an utterly, utterly typical Russian village this is, what utter, utter anarchy there is everywhere — a black goat is grazing in the street, a goat shouldn't be allowed in the street untethered, it's disorderly, it's harmful to the street and to the black goat.

Some hundred and fifty green, unshaven Germans were being herded through the absolutely happy village, on their way to a construction site, deep in the woods, after being unloaded at the station, and they still had a long way to go, and while the captain in charge of the convoy was on the phone at the village soviet working out the route they'd take, the supplies they'd need and where they'd spend the night, the German prisoners stood around picturesquely in the rain, guarded by two machine-gunners, smoking on the porch of the village soviet, themselves guarded, not by machine-gunners, but guarded by space, the feeling of defeat and joy that no one was shooting anywhere, shells weren't exploding and life-endangering commands weren't being shouted. And Franz, awaiting an unknown fate under this sky, which was new to him, picked up a stone from beside the road, pulled a rusty nail out of a paling which had come loose from the fence surrounding the village soviet, straightened out this nail on another stone and started knocking the paling back into place, and the black goat stopped nibbling the grass and started staring at Franz.

"Gut," said Franz, when he'd nailed back the paling. Real live Germans were something not to be missed. These were real ones, not just in the pictures, and little boys and the boldest of the little girls came running from all over the village and stopped at some distance from the crowd of Germans and somewhat closer to the machine-gunners. The more reckless ones pushed out to the front, and Slavka Postanogov suddenly started leaping and wheeling around, unable to contain his excitement at the sight of so many harmless enemies, and the other little boys also started leaping about in a bellicose fashion, paying no attention to the rain, which was spattering down monotonously from the sky, scattered and fine, and which was in its turn not paying attention to the unheard-of occurrence in the life of the village.

And Kostya Fomin suddenly, and unexpectedly for everyone there, but in full accord with the violence of the dance, seized a hefty clod of earth, swung back with it like a soldier throwing a grenade in the pictures and threw it at the Germans.

"Shoo off, go on!" yelled the machine-gunner, getting up, and the boys ran back.

"Mein Gott," said Franz, watching the children.

21. "Gut," said Franz

"He's been a prisoner for more than a year," said the captain to Polina, "so he already understands some Russian. He's a quiet type, a hard worker, he even seems to enjoy working."

"If he makes a nuisance of himself, I'll send him packing," said Polina.

"As far as any documents he may need are concerned," said the captain, "I'll give you a form to say he's sick and that he turned out to be a sort of relative of yours, so that for the time being, he can be left for you to keep an eye on, and I'll take him off the list, we'll say he died, so they won't start looking for him, we lose any amount of them only to have them turn up again later. When the war's over, he'll turn up again and go back home to Germany, but, in the meantime, he can do a bit of work for you, although, of course, there's no law saying they have to help around the house, but then he can go and work on the kolkhoz as well, so that everyone will be happy, and he, I should think, the happiest of all."

"I'll have a talk with him," said Polina.

"This one's the best of them," said the captain. "Well, you shouldn't be left without a man's help, should you?"

And so it happened that the captain was smart, Polina couldn't bear things as they were any longer, and Franz turned out to be peaceful and hard-working, and because of all this, Polina went up to him, this prisoner-of-war, to have a talk.

"Hello," said Polina.

"Guten Tag," said Franz.

Polina looked at him and saw his distressed face, all nervous and thin, his high forehead and light-blue eyes.

"You'll be staying here with me," said Polina.

"Gut," said Franz.

"There's the house, the children, a lot of work to do," said Polina.

"Gut," said Franz.

"Only don't you go getting any ideas," said Polina, irritated by his acquiescence. "Don't you go getting any ideas at all, you'll just be helping me, and over at the kolkhoz as well, and nothing else, so there you are."

"Gut," said Franz.

"I'll be doing whatever I can in the house as well, of course, but I find it difficult, working at the factory and at home, too, I'm all alone," said Polina. "And it'll be better for you here with me than in the camp, if you behave yourself decently, all right?"

"Gut," said Franz.

22. The Butterfly above the Meadow

However easy it is to imagine dark, gloomy town walls like a prison, with dark, gloomy stumps of stone chimneys poking above them like gravestones, and Jesus Christ walking above it all, which you can only see if your imagination is overheated, and however easy it is to imagine above all this the dark, gloomy silhouettes of black birds — carrion-crows or doves — it is quite a lot easier to see with the eyes in your head a meadow of great diversity, with butterflies above it, white, yellow and greenish cabbage butterflies, among which, from time to time, like proud eagles, beauties called peacock's eyes will wing their way, and this multitude of powdered things, so fragile you can't touch them, dances its rainbow dance above the thick grass of the meadows, stretching millions of versts across the endlessly distant spaces of Russia, from one boundless horizon to the other totally boundless horizon, and further, even further, in all directions, to all the utterly boundless horizons. But there are more white butterflies than any other, and if you want to know why, this is what you must remember:

In Russia, white is the main color, the color of birch-trees and cathedral walls, the color of dizzying bird-cherry blossom and sacred robes, the color of ermine and snow. For half the year, and sometimes longer, Russia is covered by a winter mantle, sparkling in its whiteness, beneath the moon and the sun, lighting up the deep, blue roads, the green pine branches, and the translucent sky.

The reason it's the main color is that it's made up of all the possible colors in the world — lilac and deep blue, light blue and green, yellow and orange, and red as well, so that any color or shade which can be thought up or concocted already exists in white, just as any thought which can be composed or constructed is already present in Russian thought, which is limitless, like the land which gave birth to it. This is what you must remember, when you're lying on your back, with your head in your hands and a white butterfly soars above your head. Now, blue, for example, can be amazingly beautiful, but if everything in the world were made blue — blue forest, blue flowers in blue grass, blue nose on a blue face, blue birds in a blue sky, blue hair tied up with a blue ribbon — if everything were blue, blue and only blue, then it would be completely impossible and revolting to imagine, because it would be tedious, in that monotonous blueness, to the point of screaming blue murder. But from white you can make blue eyes and golden hair and, obviously, everything else in the world, including that white sarafan which has appeared far away in the meadow, and Polina's tanned shoulders, showing from under the sarafan as she goes busily on her way.

"What am I, actually?" asked the butterfly. "Something totally insignificant, nothing in particular, all you have to do is touch me with your finger and that's the end of me, blow on me and I'll be carried off, peck me and that's the end of me. This is no life worthy of emulation. I have no knowledge of anything, so there's no point in even talking about such a trivial thing as me."

But there you lie, with your head on your hands, while the butterfly acts all modest and gives itself airs above you, and you try to grasp life, in all its variety — the variety in the meadow, for example — you try and try to grasp it, until you fall asleep, quietly, without even noticing, and forever, while the meadow goes on stretching away, for millions of versts, for millions of years, to millions of boundless horizons, encircling the absolutely happy village, and you can walk across the meadow, and walk and walk and walk, without getting tired or sick of it, but you're already asleep, you won't walk any further, you're all right now, it's the other people who'll do the walking.

You're little, of course, and all I have to do is touch you and that will be the end of you, that's certainly true, and it's hard to remember you, because most of the time, you're flying around, or else you sit folded in half, so that I have either to remember half of you, or else remember you flying. I've got a lot of time now, and I can look at you in detail, as I can everything else in the world, and I don't have to hurry after Polina, as I used to have to, when she tried to hide from me — now I'm always with her.

23. The Well with Bucket and Pole

"The well with bucket and pole is me, and the old poplar is me, too, and the forest and the river and the meadows are not you or us, but me.

"I can see everything much better now, my outlook has broadened, and very markedly, and my understanding has now deepened, because now I look at everything from above, and not from below, and I've stepped out of my own personality and it doesn't prevent me from looking at everything properly. I look, for example, at our village, through all sorts of different eyes, and I like it as much as ever, because the air above it is clean, the earth around it is green and luxuriant, thanks to all the vegetation, the river running past it is eternal and inexhaustible, and almost all the people living in it are good people, they've been living there for a long time and will live there eternally, because they will love each other and for this reason children will keep appearing in the world. I didn't think very often before, how much I liked our village, I had no time to think about it, at night I had to love Polina, so that children would appear, and by day I had to work, and then later I had to fight, both day and night. What time was there to collect my thoughts or go to see our teacher, Fyodor Mikhailovich, as he kept asking me to do, and clear up difficult questions on geography and history, or on why our village was much better than other villages."

"Fyodor Mikhailovich," said the well with bucket and pole, "was given a new house not long ago, and old Fima says that he's got two hundred books at the very least in it, all of them neatly wrapped in newspaper, and he keeps on reading and chatting with his pupils, just reading and chatting. He can't work any more, so he just teaches and chats, he's a real old man now."

"Now I've got enough time to think about what I want to, and about how I like our village."

"What is there about it to like?" said the well with bucket and pole. "Nothing special about it, take my sides, they're completely rotten and ought to be replaced."

"Well, naturally, if new sides were made, then things would be much better in the village."

"Lots of the houses are old and delapidated, and too cramped, too, lots of them are too cramped," said the well with bucket and pole.

"Well, naturally, it would be even better if new, roomy ones were put up, instead of the old delapidated ones."

"What is there about it to like?" said the well with the bucket and pole. "Look at all those women who have no one to love them. Old Fima says, it doesn't worry me, my time is over, but it's no good for the young ones, it's harmful to the health."

"All this whining and squeaking just reveals your bad character," said Mikheyev. "You can't penetrate the essence of things because of your character. You've got a skull buried inside you and a string of pearls caught up down there, and you think about this and feel proud that such secrets are concealed inside you. I've had enough of talking to you, I'm going down to the river, where Polina and I first embraced that time."

"If they replace my shaft they'll find the pearls," the well with bucket and pole called after him. "They'll take it away to the bank, and who knows what they'll do with it there. They might exchange it for foreign currency, or they might make a gift of it to some African princess."

24. By the River where Polina and I First Embraced

"I must say, river, how like Polina you are from above, and that bend of yours is like the curve in Polina's neck, when she turned her face away, and her hair flowed across the grass in bright waves, I didn't notice, from down there, that you were so like her. Swimming in your depths, river, are perch, with red fins and dark stripes on their backs, and resentfully pouting lips under round eyes. Above your blueness, river, floats a blue sky, flowing in the opposite direction to you, and scattering stars into you at night. You run past the village, from Postanogov's bathhouse to the hoary old man's dwelling; you run, although you're not running away from anywhere, and you stay in place, true to your riverbanks, from those three maples which stand opposite the bathhouse to that willow which is opposite the hoary old man's place, and you're true to that forest, which lies between them and stretches even further. And now it's evening again, and from the gardens the sound of songs of an amorous nature is being carried, although they're now being sung, not by our friends, but the children of yesterday. And mine are among them, they've turned out strong and healthy, and Andrei and Klara's daughters are among them — Faith, Hope and little Charity — none of them married, yet."

"I don't like it," said the river. "People don't meet on my banks as much as they used to, and yesterday Faith came and sat there deep in thought till very late, but completely alone."

"Thinking all alone is a temporary state of affairs for her," said Mikheyev. "She'll soon be thinking in a twosome, only they'll leave here for Dikson Island, and there they'll keep each other warm and give birth to a little daughter, a new Faith."

"There aren't any rivers like me on Dikson Island," said the river.

"Her hair used to flow across the grass in bright waves," said Mikheyev. "Thank you, river."

25. Why Don't You Leave, Franz?

"I don't suppose you're completely German," said Polina.

"Was ist das — not completely German?" asked Franz.

"Do you remember I said to you there was the house, and the children, and a lot of work to do, and you said Gut, and I told you not to go getting any ideas, but just help me and you said Gut, and I told you to behave yourself properly, and you said Gut, that is to say, what I meant was, that you shouldn't make a nuisance of yourself, or look on me as a woman, and even to that you said Gut. And you fixed the roof, and the fence, and taught the children how to help, and you went to the kolhoz and did lots of work of different kinds, and you were honest and straight-forward, so that everyone took a liking to you, and lots of people even came to us for advice, and you helped everyone. And you didn't make a nuisance of yourself. You said Gut, and that's the way you did everything! No tricks, no cheating. That's why you're not completely German."

"No," said Franz. "I'm completely German, and my father and mother were completely German, too.."

"Do you remember how old Fima came and said that her son was at the war, too, so you should go and live at her place now, and you looked at me, and I said to old Fima that you were a relative of mine, and that the fact that her son was at the war had nothing to do with anything. But you still went over to her place and dug up her potatoes for her, and cured Yegorovna's cow and taught the Postanogovs to brew beer."

"I learnt them to brew beer after the war," said Franz.

"And you didn't look on me as a woman, you said Gut, and you meant it, for goodness sake," said Polina. "But the village was a bit doubtful about who you belonged to — everyone, or just me, and when people started talking about this in front of you, you would look at me, and you'd look and look, in such a way that once I couldn't stand it any longer and shouted at them not to keep on at you — you were my husband, was that clear? But you weren't my husband then, just my distant relative and a good man."

"He wasn't making the beer in the right way, he doesn't take enough time over it," said Franz. "He wasn't letting the wort settle, and he used to put vodka instead of wine into the leaven, as it's called."

"I wanted a boy," said Polina. "And I got two little girls. Is it my lot in life, to give birth to twins?"

"I think nature is the cause," said Franz. "It's good to have two at once. If you wanted to have more children, you might get two boys. A pity not to try."

"Are you going over to Postanogovs today?" asked Polina.

"Yes," said Franz. "They've sent him another notice. They've found me, again. How many times is that, since the war?"

"Five," said Polina. "Five times they've found you, in twelve years."

"They do their work well," said Franz. "I'm a long way away, but they've found me five times. Different organizations look for me, and each one finds me."

As chairman of the village soviet, Postanogov occupied a prominent position in the village, but even though this was so, his table stood in the corner without a tablecloth and without an oil-cloth and moreover, under icons, and what's even more, there was a lamp burning in front of the icons, while the kerosene lamp, on the table, had no glass and made the faces of his guests all sooty, as if they weren't swarthy enough as it was, and their eyes would flash in their dark faces, and on the table, there was a big jug of beer and some glasses. There were six guests, sitting on benches alongside the table, under the icons, because Postanogov's wife was a religious woman, and he hadn't been able to do anything about it for forty years, despite the enormous length of time he'd spent in the party, and his wife's faith left her no time for embroidering the table cloth, brightening up their daily life or buying new glass for the lamp.

"I don't understand, Franz Karlovich," said Postanogov, "why you don't leave. Of course, we don't want you to go away, you're a first-class worker, you don't drink, we appreciate having you, you're not a careerist, but you've got your own country, it's capitalist, I know, but all the same, it's yours, and you've got your family and roots there, your relatives. That's what I don't understand."

"It's hard to understand," said the young Fomin, pouring himself some beer. "It's almost totally impossible for a Russian to understand."

"My family lives near Magdeburg," said Franz. "They're different now. My wife, no doubt, has a new husband. Everything used to be very orderly on my farm, and I expect everything is now. Everything has always been well-run and peaceful and that's they way it goes on being. Here, I've got a new family, a new wife, two daughters of my own, my wife's two sons, things aren't too orderly, so there's a lot of thinking to be done about how it's possible for there to be so little order, yet people live and some of them are very good people. I'd like to know how long it's going to go on like this and how it will change, and how order is going to come out of the disorder, and when. I can't leave, these are things I really want to know. And my wife is a very good person, and I've got fine children, I don't want to leave them, either. I was a prisoner-of-war, and she took me into her house like a relative, which isn't an orderly thing to do, either, but the captain and she and you created that disorder and I'm grateful to you for it. Germans wouldn't have done it, there's anarchy wherever you look, yet I don't want to leave."

"You're criticizing our present reality, Franz Karlovich," said Postanogov. "Why is that?"

"No, he's not," said Postanogov's neighbor. "The man's thinking aloud, that's something we should appreciate."

"My opinion is that he should be allowed to live here with us," said the younger Fomin.

"No one's arguing with that," said Postanogov. "If there were anarchy wherever you looked, Franz Karlovich, then we'd have all died off, long ago, but we're alive, I'd like you to understand that."

"Ich verstehe," said Franz.

26. The Scarecrow in the Garden and Its Dreams

The moon shone under its cap into its primeval eyes while all around it the sunflowers rocked their black heads.

A cow, at home somewhere nearby, mooed sleepily, fish splashed in the river and circles floated across the water with the speed of the current.

There's a need to tell, all the same, what this one absolutely happy village looks like as a whole. Just imagine a blue, blue river and a blue, blue sky...but no, you can't imagine that right now because night is lying over the land and the sky at this time is not at all blue, although it *is* beautiful.

"I used to talk to you a lot once," said Mikheyev, "but there were lots of things we didn't talk out. I was always in a hurry to go somewhere, there were lots of things to do."

"Well, I'm not in a hurry," said the scarecrow. "There was never anywhere for me to hurry off to."

"I'm not in a hurry now, either," said Mikheyev. "The boundless village lies around me."

"Actually, in the fall and winter I don't have anything to do at all," said the scarecrow. "I have dreams, remarkable dreams. For example, this winter I had a very long dream. First I dreamed of a bell ringing and a long, long church procession which was making its way along beside the river. Carts were squeaking, the cows tied to the wagons were mooing, and dogs were barking as they ran along beside this string of carts or was it a procession? Everyone was in it, all of them people I know — the Fomins, the Postanogovs, old Yegorovna and her family, and old Fima and the children. Even the hoary old man was walking along there at the end, unwillingly, behind the very last cart — he'd walk for a bit and then stop, doubtfully. And the bells rang out in every voice you can think of."

"You must have something from the church wound around you, if you dreamt of church bells," said Mikheyev. "Perhaps your jacket was once worn by a sexton. Why else would you have dreams like that?"

"The procession crossed the river and then from somewhere appeared a hill, a tall one, with green slopes and a road winding up to the top. And on top of the hill your

Polina was standing with Ilya and Alyosha beside her, tall and sturdy, just as in real life."

"You dreamt that because of the talks we had," said Mikheyev.

"Polina was wearing the white dress with a red belt she wore to the wedding party, and Ilya and Alyosha were wearing something silver, I couldn't make out exactly what. And the whole procession started to go up the hill towards them, slowly, I must have been dreaming of it going.up that hill for a whole month. Then I was woken up by the wind, it made the roof rattle, it was hard for me to get to sleep again, most of the dream I missed while the wind was rattling the roof. Then I dreamt of an empty field, with a whole lot of words written on it in white pebbles, only I couldn't read what they were — grass had sprung up between the pebbles and I couldn't make out the words."

"You've got a railwayman's cap on, there are words picked out in white pebbles beside the railway track and you saw them in your dreams," said Mikheyev.

"And I dreamt about you in that field," said the scarecrow. "Only for some reason you were sad and started telling me about how deeply you loved our village but how you could now see a lot of things you hadn't been able to see before, and how you wanted the earth to be more fertile and the herds more numerous, how you wanted there to be more people and more children, too, and the houses to be brighter and roomier, and people to be less cunning and think less about their own advantage. That was when I had to tell you that the things you wanted were impossible."

"Why impossible?" asked Mikheyev. "These are all quite simple, easy things. What's impossible, for example, about the forest being even greener? It's very simple to see the whole of our boundless village beautiful, without spot. Houses standing one here, one there, amidst luxuriant gar-

dens, covered in hops, ivy and other vines, with clean windows in them, and neat furniture, and healthy people
living in them, going about their business sensibly, intelli-
gently and with a sense of humor, cheerily and with a sense
of dignity, caring about each other and loving the earth
beneath them. That's easy to imagine, so what's impossible
about it? And the difference between that and what exists
isn't particularly great, because if it were particularly great,
life would long ago have come to an end, but it hasn't."

"Don't you understand that people are different — they
have different desires and almost everyone wants to receive
and not give at all?" said the scarecrow.

"The reason you're dreaming that it's impossible is that
those buttons you've got on have been cut off an officer's
jacket," said Mikheyev.

"Well, you ask the earth if you don't believe me," said the
scarecrow.

27. Mikheyev Talks to the Earth

"Why is it, earth," asked Mikheyev, "that if you imagine that
there are houses standing one here, one there on you, rich
and fertile as you are, all with clean windows in them, neat
furniture, and the people living in them healthy and cheer-
ful and so on, then the more you think about it and imagine it, the less clearly you can see it, as if the light were
becoming brighter than necessary, brighter and brighter,
so that the light extinguishes everything and you can't
make out anything except light, can't see anything at all
except light, and can't take a close look at the details of it
all?"

"No, not a close one," said the earth.

"You can make out the odd separate detail and imagine it to yourself as clearly as anything, so that particular detail is a happy, good one, but is it because of the light that you can't make out other details right next to that one?"

"Yes, because of the light," said the earth.

"You're bearing upon yourself one absolutely happy village," said Mikheyev.

"Yes, I am," said the earth.

"Well, there are things in it that should be improved, improved a lot, you know that yourself, but when things have improved altogether, there is just light and nothing else, and we go blind from the light, and like blind men heaven knows what things we do in the dark."

"Talk to me," said the earth. "Talk."

But for some reason Mikheyev suddenly fell silent, as if he had lost track of his thoughts, as if he were staring fixedly at something or watching something which was both moving further away and closer and closer at the same time. He was staring quite calmly at something flying towards him or flying away in a straight line, and human voices had become inaudible, as had the splashing of the river at the riverbank, the sound of the leaves on the poplars, and the evening cries of the loud-speaker in the center of the village. And in the midst of this deafening silence the earth said without reproach, although also without approval:

"Raindrops on a hot summer's day disappear from the leaf beside the road, leaving on it traces of dirt and dust. Sometimes night catches the villager beside the river unawares, and the adult remembers his childish fears if the night is moonless, and in the distance there are rolls of thunder, and it is airless, and there's no coolness in the air, and lying beside him on the sand is his fisherman's net, and in it there are a few small-fry flapping feebly, unwanted and forgotten. The abyss of air turns dark, something unseen, concealed from the eyes, takes place in it, and only a few flashes of lightning attempt to light everything up, but they don't succeed — electricity is powerless to do this. And the approach of night, Mikheyev, is hard for me to take, and there is nothing in the world for which it isn't hard, and no one for whom it isn't hard. That's why people are in a hurry to fall asleep for the night, so as to sleep through their fear and last till the morning."

Mikheyev stayed silent, all that happened was that his eyes started to look as if he were about to cry, but couldn't, not having learned how to while he was alive.

The earth was also silent for a while, waiting for an answer, but it could wait no longer and started to talk to him again:

"I don't know who will last to the morning, Mikheyev. Come into my maternal damp and warmth, together we'll listen and wait."

Mikheyev shook his head and returned to immobility.

"Well, don't if you don't want to," said the earth. "It happens sometimes, I won't be offended. But listen, there's someone coming. Imagine, on a night like this and they're not asleep with their eyes tightly closed, but their eyes are open as if it were possible to make anything out, and they're walking in the darkness towards the black river, and they'll whisper together and then fall silent, and then she'll cry out with happiness and pain, and then they'll start whispering together again, and suddenly, Mikheyev, you have the miracle that they love each other, just as you and Polina loved each other. There's one of her tears rolling down — can you see it, Mikheyev, a pure tear. There you are, she's understood everything in advance and given her forgiveness — can you see, Mikheyev? Look, look,

Mikheyev, he stroked her hair!"

Now there came a proper roll of thunder in the sky, breaking up the silence, and heavy rain started ringing on the leaves, and the whispering couple hid themselves away somewhere, and Mikheyev lifted up his head and stayed standing there on the now silent earth and the rain kept falling, falling, falling on his wet face and closed eyes. And through the rain, or inside him, could be heard something between a refrain and church-bells.

Boris Vakhtin (1930-1981), a sinologist and translator of Chinese literature, was a member of an unofficial group of writers in Leningrad called "Urbanites." His works circulated widely in the underground press. *The Sheepskin Coat* first appeared in Russian in *Metropol,* a literary almanac of uncensored literature which was published in the West in 1979. *An Absolutely Happy Village* was also published in the West in 1982 in the collection *Dve povesti* (*Two Novellas*) (Ardis Publishers).